Mother Guru

D1528266

Mother Guru

Savitri Love Poems

Poems by Red Hawk

HOHM PRESS
Chino Valley, Arizona

© 2014, Robert Moore

All rights reserved. No part of this book may be reproduced in any manner without written permission from the publisher, except in the case of quotes used in critical articles and reviews.

Cover Design: Adi Zuccarello

Interior Design and Layout: Kubera Book Design, Prescott, Arizona

Library of Congress Cataloging-in-Publication Data

Red Hawk.
  [Poems. Selections]
  Mother Guru : Savitri Love Poems : Poems / by Red Hawk.
    pages cm
  ISBN 978-1-935387-84-8 (trade pbk. : acid-free paper)
  I. Title.
  PS3568.E295A6 2014
  811'.54--dc23
                                2014012647

Hohm Press
P.O. Box 4410
Chino Valley, AZ 86323
800-381-2700
http://www.hohmpress.com

This book was printed in the U.S.A. on recycled, acid-free paper using soy ink.

Te Dominus Amat
(The Love of God)

ॐ

For Mister Lee, the Beloved Guru &
for His Father in Heaven,
Yogi Ramsuratkumar

in loving & faithful gratitude

ॐ

"You, in Your great Mercy
and infinite generosity, in
Your Radiant Grace and
Motherly care for Your infants,
have given us Your Name,
and how true, how true, for
it is not other than You."

–Lee Lozowick, *Intimate Secrets of a True Heart Son,*

Contents

PROLOGUE:
Mother Guru

Mother Guru

Oh the wind, it howls all day long today
without ceasing, like a small child
who has lost his mother in a rail station
the way I have lost You.
I am your small child Dearest
sitting here in my room in the dome
reading and writing, thinking of You
like a lost child who thinks
only of his mother. He weeps for her
and thinks how she softly wipes his tears
with her hair, wets her skirt with her lips
and washes the tears from his face
Dearest, the way you dry my tears.

All of a sudden
there is a loud bang and the dome door
flies open. Though the doorway
appears to be empty
I am not fooled Dearest, I sense
that You are standing there
wrapped in the rags of the wind,
hair on fire with Sunlight,
blue eyes birthing the starry worlds.
My heart leaps at the first loud bang
like a lost child who spies his mother
across the infinitely vast rail station.

I am a shy man, but You are a skilled
and gentle Mother dear Master; I know
it is blasphemy to say You are my Mother,
it is crazy to even confess it and yet
Master, You are my Mother: You

(continues)

feed me, You clothe me, You bathe me,
You hold me, You may be Father to the world
and to every other living thing, but
You cannot fool me for a moment;
no one knows his Mother
like a lost child in a rail station
who catches hold of her skirt at last.

Part i:

The Body of Christ

The Body of Christ

The highest Beings create a fourth body,
an Angelic body also known as
the Body of Christ; this
is the function of the Sangha,
to become the Guru's immortal body
so that His Dharma never dies.

Oh you saviours, you fishers of men,
arise now and trek towards Bethlehem;
our task is to keep alive His Dharma
and in so doing, to work out our karma,
always in service to our Lord
and by our actions to become His Word.

By our deeds He will be known
and by our behavior His Way will be shown.
At the Guru's death, either the Body awakens
or His Work in the world is forsaken
and His light grows dim.
In every breath, remember Him.

Now we are cast upon the waters
as bread to feed the fishes.
We must not hoard what we have been given,
but give to others as He who is now in Heaven
gave to us; those are His wishes
and His wish is all that matters.

Death Is A Favor To Us
(Hafiz)

That Death is a favor to us, Mister Lee
has shown us beyond the shadow
of Death; His play of the Miraculous
everywhere we go makes even
the chattering mind have grave doubts.

He inverts rainbows so they smile
down upon us, He runs circles
of light around the Sun, He gives
a little man like me the Faith
of a true-believer while

leaving my doubt intact, a neat
and hilarious trick which marries
the impermanence of form with the
lightness of Being. The Master pours
His Wine into our cup endlessly

and invites us to be as drunk
as the Saints in His Tavern, who
laugh and raise Heaven every night
over the hilarious trick of the Human form
and the favor of Death to reveal the Master

behind the curtain of flesh,
pulling the strings,
pouring the wine,
pulling a Living Being out of
the empty hat of the body;

the Master has Death up His sleeve.

The Good Son

The disciple Thomas tells us that Jesus said,
Find the man who was not born of woman
and fall down on your face and
worship him,
for He is your Father.

Mister Lee found such a one
in Yogi Ramsuratkumar and
he fell down on his face before Him
and worshipped Him as his Father.

I am not one like Mister Lee, though
I see that He too is born of no woman
and I can do nothing other than to
fall down on my face before Him;

however, I worship Him as my Mother.
Oh my dear Mother, I pray that
You will do to me what Your Father
had done to You:

make me a good Son, Mother.

Anything But God

When you meet the Guru, the whole world
is in flames, the heart is on fire
and the mind claws to regain its hold
like a rat flushed down a sewer.

There were 30 of us gathered in a room
to be with the Guru and hear Him speak.
One guy had a question about his anger; some
questions won't let go of you, they break

you down, they rip and tear. Then you stand
or run, depending on how bad you want to know.
This guy ran, disappeared; God is a risk the mind
cannot take. Later we asked him, Where'd you go?

I got bored, he said, went to Hooters.
Once the Guru gets you, nothing else matters:
not tits, or ass, or bored wife-beaters,
not global polluters, government looters, or schoolyard
        shooters.

But until that time, anything in the world is better
than bowing down and loving the Guru as your Mother.

Homeless Wandering Beggar

My only home is beneath the Guru's shawl
which is my sole refuge; His Dharma clothes me,
His Sangha feeds me. When the Guru's shawl
is in motion, I move; when it is still, I am

huddled beneath it. There is no home
but the Guru, everything else is transient,
everything else falls down, becomes dust.
Only the Guru endures.

His Dharma is the shirt I wear,
I put on His Dharma like a pair of pants,
I place my feet in His Dharma,
I carry His Dharma like a begging bowl

which He is always filling up.
This Earth has no home for me
but the Guru, who is my body,
my breath, my blood, my life.

Where there is a desert,
the Guru is the blowing sand;
where there is a mountain pass,
the Guru is the melting snow.

Do you understand that I have lost everything
and found the Guru? Do you not see
that I am nothing, that the Guru owns this
nothing and He makes of it what He wishes?

(continues)

Come, fill my bowl with Your breath,
cover this flesh with Your garments,
lay Your dear hands on this brow,
let Your Grace rain upon this upturned face.

The Barren Woman's Orphan Child

Oh my Beloved Mother Guru, by your Grace
you have given me the gift of feeling shame.
I am so grateful; it reminds me always of You.

I bow down and kiss your dear feet and
beg you Dearest to allow me to keep feeling
this shame which you have bestowed upon me.

Thank God I can still feel. I who believed
I had no feeling left in me Blessed Mother, found
Your shame left on my doorstep, as a barren woman

finds an orphan and with a grateful heart cares for it
with humility and forbearance, her joy neither
proud nor foolish, without boast or show; she

simply worships the child she is given
and provides for it with all her heart, every day
giving thanks and bowing down before it,

washing it and kissing its dear feet.

How Did You Come To Me?

How, how, how is it possible
that the Lord of the Universe
stood before me and I saw Him not?
There is something that does not pass away
and It stood before me as a Bad Poet
and Arrogant Fool; that which transcends
all time and space, which knows us
before we are born and holds us
in Its kind Regard after we die,
was right there before me. I knelt
before Him and gave Him gifts, I sat
before Him in the Tavern of Broken Hearts
and spoke to Him, laughed with Him,
took kindness from His hands and still
I did not see Him.
Oh my dear Lord, You came to me
as a man called Mister Lee, a man
playing in a Blues band; how, how, how
could that be the Lord of the Universe
dressed in rags of light and singing
with a broken, ragged voice, making
bad jokes in Holy places, acting a fool,
raining down upon us every conceivable kindness,
showering us with Grace and Mercy?
Oh my dear Lord, how could I not see You,
how could I not fall down and worship You,
how could I not adore You and give all,
all that I owned for one glimpse of Your face?
Mother Guru forgive me, for I did not know
it was possible that the Lord of the Universe could
love a foolish man the likes of me.

A Refusal To Praise My Master

I come from the Demon world where sickness
runs like a septic river in the veins and sorrow
is the milk the infant is suckled with. Here we
do not praise the Master, we blame and curse
what is good and right; in this world we insist
upon our right to do harm; we suck smoke into the body,
we massacre the trees, we poison the water, hit
our children. So do not expect praise from me
dear Master; You who are my every breath and
waking thought, You

who pray unceasingly and without rest for the healing
of all Beings, will not hear a single note of praise issue forth
from these parched and bleeding lips; we do not
praise the Master in the Demon world, we shoot
and rape and scorn, we curse and kill and steal and
mourn, we laugh and weep and scoff, we are wasted
and torn, but we do not praise here, neither the dying nor
the newly born. We do not praise Your dearest
loving eyes, those worn and haunting lights of Heaven;
we do not praise

the One who stands as news of God before us; we do not
praise the Dharma King, the bearer of the Law which we
will not follow; we do not praise the glory of Your name; we
do not bow before your marvelous countenance and worship
the unceasing devotion and unconditional adoration of
Your love for Your Father Yogi Ramsuratkumar; we will not
bow down, we will not acknowledge, we will not worship, we
will not follow, we will not praise Your majesty; we insist,
we demand, we complain, we condemn, we do not
praise the Master in the Demon world.

I Do Not Love the Guru

It's not my gift, to love the Guru.
Others have been given that gift,
not me.

My gift is to love the Guru's Dharma,
His teaching and the way
He manifests that teaching,

His every move, every word, the look
in His eye, the way He looks at me,
how He sits, the way He dresses,

His walk, how He stands composed, steady
and serene, the way a Blue Heron
will stand in a still pond

among the Lilies, one leg raised,
motionless, its reflection rippled
by a breeze, its feathers ruffled

in the wind, but no movement, no struggle,
no blinking of the eye.
I do not love the Heron,

I love the way He is in the pond,
the still point
around which a world slowly turns,

the fixed Attention holding the world in place.

Getting My Hands Dirty

Yogi Ramsuratkumar lived on the town garbage dump
in Tiruvannamalai for 25 years,
and for many of those years every time

He went out on the street the village thugs,
young boys angry that they had been
cheated by life and without

any other recourse, beat the Spiritual Master and
left Him lying bleeding in the street where
He only Blessed and forgave them. This occurred

after His enlightenment for which He endured
unspeakable suffering, living in a tiny room
with snakes and scorpions and white ants

crawling all over His body and stinging Him until
the body was nearly dead and
this is the man I refuse to bow down to because

doing so might entail for me
some personal inconvenience, some small sacrifice
which is more than I am willing to put up with;

I don't want to get my hands dirty.

Send A Fool To Catch an Idiot

Oh Mother Guru you don't fool this Idiot,
though it is subtle as the wind
wearing away the mountain,

You are wearing down this Idiot,
the Body of Habits is stumbling, slowly
grinding to a halt. Oh Mother Guru

You do not escape this Idiot's attention,
I see You in every leaf, under every stone,
behind the eyes of every pretty woman;

I see how You follow me, as its shadow
follows the dull Ox through the market place.
Everywhere I turn, there You are Mother Guru.

I have ½ Your wit, none of Your elegance, but
arrogance enough for both of us so I can
relieve You of that burden and

I have foolishness enough to make the whole world
stumble and fall down like one on fire and drunk
with Your Love.

You do not fool me dearest, though I am
slow as a leaf afloat in a still pond, still
I am a goner, done in by Your Love.

You call Yourself an Arrogant Fool.
Isn't that just like the Great God:
send a Fool to catch an Idiot.

Pennies From Heaven

Some guys have all the luck.
I'm one of them.
I stumbled across this Jew
who happened to be the Son of God;
no not that Jew,
the other one, the one who
lived in Arizona and stayed the hell away
from the Pharisees and Sadducees and
pharmacies and wannabes.
You can nail the Son of God once, but
the next time He will sell you something
you didn't even know you wanted and
at a price you cannot afford but
cannot afford to pass up. So once I found
the Son of God, I stuck close to Him so
the luck would rub off, like a shoeshine boy
who follows a rich man and picks up the pennies
he leaves scattered in his wake. And
that's exactly what the Jew does, He
leaves pennies for me everywhere I go,
in the most unlikely places and
exactly when I need His support the most,
there will be a penny at my feet, where
there was nothing a moment ago, pennies
from Heaven. I've got a big jar full of them;
pick up enough pennies and pretty soon
you've got a dollar. I've learned to pay
close attention because He will drop one on me
when I least expect it and I don't want Him
to get the wrong message: If this fool can't be
bothered with a penny, then I won't bother him
with a million dollars.

Just Follow

To follow is the
easiest thing in the world,
Mister Lee said to a group of disciples
gathered around Him.
Why don't you
just follow?
I love to follow, He continued.
It is the most easeful,
peaceful thing to do. Instead
you have all your opinions,
ideas, your needs. Go here,
do that, do this,
requests, I need, I want,
always trying to
control
everything.
It's terrible,
He said and
for a moment the disciples
grouped around Him were silent.

Then one of them spoke up: Why
don't we go over there for chai?
No, not there, another said,
it's too crowded.

Entering the Guru's World

First You brought me wounded to my knees,
then lay me broken, face down in the dirt.
You heard my begging, heartfelt, desperate pleas,
responded to my weeping from the hurt.

The moment that I let the Guru in,
then all the garbage from my life rose up;
every dirty, stinking little sin
was poured into my foul and bitter cup.

I drank it down, that fatal poison brew
then lay upon my dark and dying bed
and cried aloud into the dark for You,
while all the demons in my body bled.

The Guru is the greatest mystery,
His kindness is the Sacred Heart of Grace,
but first I must die to my history
so He may restore my original face.

Wise child is born when old torment is killed
and in its place a spark is lit in us
which catches fire until the Heart is filled,
consumed in Love and radiant in Trust.

What We Can Give To Our Children

A man once came to Mister Lee terribly upset.
His son had been raped and he
did not know what to do.

Pray for him, Mister Lee said.
When your children are in trouble in their life,
get down on your knees

and pray for them.
Physically pray for them.
Tell them you love them and

you're there for them but
you must let your children
do their own Work.

They must
do their own Work.
If you don't let them

do their own Work
they will become
cripples.

If we don't,
we do them a disservice,
we rescue them,

we do the Work for them
and they don't
grow.

The Remains of Our Children
(Carlos Castaneda)

We get such small leavings,
the torn remnants of their lives.
Once we've planted our own bad seeds
in their fertile gardens,
we are left with our inner grieving,
our remorse, which the Soul uses as It strives
to gather all that It needs
to escape this life before it hardens
into darkness. Perhaps we need this thieving,
stealing from our children what they have to give
us, taking all that breathes and bleeds,
leaving them to build anew, begging their pardons

for draining them of their life-force
so we could escape the slaughter on a fresh horse.

The Travel Prayer

Given by Mister Lee for His disciples to repeat when
they are traveling, it is one more item of Grace
in a world fraught with peril.

Here's how it works. My daughter and
her young son Iain are on the long road home
from Montana when for no discernible reason

she pulls over to get water and food when she
doesn't need either. As she gets back in,
she remembers the Travel Prayer in her wallet,

gets it out, reads it aloud and goes on her way.
Minutes later she is doing 70 on a 2-lane road when
a woman turns directly into her oncoming path,

then stops when she realizes her error, rather
than accelerating through to clear the way.
My daughter brakes hard and swerves right, but

the woman, made idiot by terror, then decides to
complete the turn, all of this in mili-seconds, and now
in one last desperate maneuver my daughter swerves

left to hit her sideways rather than head on. The crash
is deafening, the airbags explode and now daughter's car
is thrown across oncoming traffic, a 30-foot drop on one side,

a 15-foot drop on the other, and she is
blinded by the airbags, desperately braking, and
can see nothing. Finally,

the bags deflate, the car comes to rest, she has
managed to avoid both ditches and oncoming traffic,
and she and her son are without a scratch.

The machinery of Grace is unfathomable; Oh Merciful,
my daughter and grandson live, they live; we must simply
bow down and pray, as if our lives depended upon it.

Tempering the Love

The great Master George Gurdjieff rarely revealed
His softness, His kindness and compassion, His love
to His students; He did not want them to get lost
in the heart any more than in the head. Instead

He wanted them to focus on His transmission
of Dharma Practice.
Last night I was in a small, intimate space
with 50 people for a talk by Mister Lee.

The mood was infused with kindness, a side
of Mister Lee He rarely displays in public.
You could see people going soft.
Suddenly Mister Lee says, I'm going to

get in trouble for this, and He launches into
a shocking story of Holy men molesting small boys.
There is a shift of mood in the room, everything
is no longer soft and cuddly, now there is a price

to be paid. There is an almost audible crash
between people's dreams and the reality of the Guru.
This happens often in His company, and
when their ass is on fire, most people

kill the Guru, pour His blood on the fire
to save their ass.

Making A Tool For the Guru
(in response to your lovely note)

Make me a book, He said, and
make it brief and simple, one that
anyone can understand;
do it in 3 months flat

so we can print it in the Fall.
That was all.
I did as I was told,
though it seemed impossible to hold

attention steady on such a large task
and not yield to doubt and fear.
My only hope was every day to ask
the Guru for help and with my inner ear

to listen for it when it arrived.
Nothing of what I thought I knew survived
the melting down and giving way;
help came through determination to obey,

just that simple, the dogged practice of daily
sitting before the Guru with folded hands
and begging to be shown the way. With unfailing
Grace the Guru took pity on me, and on demand

the words came like a merciful blessing shower
from the Guru's almighty benevolent power.
What's required is 1 part worship, 3 parts sweat,
and going ever-deeper into the Guru's debt.

Like a storm-tossed sailor, in the Guru's game
my only hope is to cling to the Guru's Name.

Often the Greatest Help Is Not-Doing

After blowing several obvious chances
to help my Guru, once by His direct request,
finally my prayer was to be of some use to Him,
no matter how small or seemingly insignificant.
Like nearly everything my mind imagines, nothing
unfolds in the way I had it figured.

Because I loved her sweet voice and
the way she bled out the tunes which
Mister Lee wrote for her, I was inspired
to write some torch songs, some blues
for her, which I did.
None of them amounted to much, but

I took them to Mister Lee and told Him
what I was up to. He said,
Writing the songs is one of the few things
which gives me real pleasure.
That is all He said. He
did not ask me not to do it, did not say

that to do so would rob Him
of one of His few pleasures;
no plea, no justification, no excuse, but
in that moment I saw my opportunity,
the thing I had prayed for.
Without regret or self pity,

I never wrote another song.

My Sweet Lord Guru

Daily He sat before us and
allowed us to wear Him away like
steady wind and hard rain
alter the stone. He disappeared
before our eyes into God,
becoming what is meant by
Human Being. His face grew
lined and ancient with the years
and the gravity of the Good Shepherd's task:
He must lead us bawling and bleating,
eager to give ourselves to the first hungry wolf,
into the slaughterhouse of love where
we will be roasted and consumed by God.

Once when I walked into the Ashram office
He rose from His chair when He saw me
and He came to me and embraced me,
held me close and said,
Welcome, in my ear. Then
He stepped back and said,
If I did not have a sore throat,
I would kiss you.

You see how He hammers on my heart
with His gentle kindness, how relentless
like waves crashing upon a shore
is His tender mercy.
As he disappeared and God emerged,
we could see just what Our Creator was made of:
it is kindness upon kindness
as far as the eyes can see,

(continues with stanza break)

patience as vast as the unnumbered starry worlds,
and a love which burns as the Sun of all Suns;
it consumes everything.
Many are drawn to the Light,
but precious few can stand the heat.

Pleasure In Simple Things

The old ways do not inspire;
I take the greatest pleasure
in sitting by the fire;
Your Presence is the real treasure

and nothing else serves half so well.
I write a note, I listen to the rain,
I stay in the present where You dwell;
no thinking or desire is worth the pain

of losing You when my Attention leaves.
I walk, I stack the firewood on the porch;
in simple things my Heart no longer grieves.
The present is Your home, it is Your church,

I go to worship and adore You there.
It's such a simple secret You've concealed,
so people go on looking everywhere
but in the moment where You stand revealed.

So I live only in the here and now
where little men like me may stand and serve,
may feed You with Attention and a bow,
and give You the devotion You deserve.

Each simple movement is a kind of prayer
when full Attention's given to the deed,
so smallest act is done with Loving care;
it's on Attention You and Father feed.

The Easy Way Out

I am one who always looked
for the easy way out.
Of course, it turns out that
there is no easy way out for anything
or anyone in this world, but
that never mattered to the mind.
It clung to the illusion of the easy way.

So when the Guru said He wanted to come
to my town to sell antiquities and
would I arrange it, I said yes.
Then the shit train pulled into the station.
The mind went into its terror, looking
under every dog pile for some way out.
The only thing it came up with, after

days of discarding one impossible scenario
after another was, if I die then
I can get out of this.
That was it, the bottom line. The only problem
was that it could not imagine the compassion
or the skillful means of the Guru.
Weeks before His visit, I am told that

He cannot come. He is too sick.
Thoughts are so easy that I forget
they have power to shape reality,
power to do real harm: Did the Guru
take my wish to die upon Himself?
It gave the easy way out
a whole new meaning.

Taking Care of Business

Yogi Ramsuratkumar gives out bananas
at His Darshan. Disciples come to His feet,
He gives them a banana, they peel and eat it,

He takes the peel in His hands and disposes
of it. There is much speculation about
what this means but most agree He is

taking a burden we cannot carry for ourselves.
But it is not like that with Mister Lee:
He goes to His Father's feet, takes the banana,

peels and quickly folds the skin, eats the banana,
puts the skin in His pocket,
does His own dirty work.

Most of us are glad to let others do our dirty work
for us so that we can spend our lives
feeling offended by the deeds of others and

never offended by our own self importance.
We gladly eat the banana and
let someone else dispose of the peel.

No Personal Life

What about me? is the question
the ego never stops asking because
that is the only thing it knows but

it is not the concern of the Master.
Mister Lee has no social life, only
Work opportunities for His students,

no free time, only
obligation to the Work, no
vacation, nothing laid back, no

relaxation except observation.
I see how He is consumed by the Work
in a way that is not sane or rational;

if you want sane and rational you have to
stick with your personal hell
no matter how bad it hurts, who

it ruins, it's better to be a
free agent in hell than
to serve God, anything

is better than that.
Just look at Mister Lee, no
social life;

who would want that?

Tattooed And Gurued

He is 63
just like me, but
that is the only similarity.

He is fiercely tattooed across
shoulders, chest and back, and is the boss
of 2 touring bands. Profit and loss

are His only concerns;
everything is for sale, He always turns
a profit. On stage with the bands, He burns

the crowds the way a lightning strike
scorches the spine of a tree. With mic
in hand he uses it like

shamans use a Birch wand to pierce the veil
between the worlds and set sail
upon the turbulent human heart. Without fail

He brings us safely to the further shore
and briefly we aren't human anymore;
with haunted longing we shed the flesh we wore

and shake out folded angel's wings,
moist and wrinkled like all newborn things;
we lift and circle, transformed as He sings.

Standing By One's Word

Our words have become furiously cheap
and curiously without value as we keep
speaking them with no thought or feeling
for their cost to self or others, thus they are stealing
our spirits right from under our noses.
Real honor in a human being supposes
a thoughtful reticence, a reluctance to speak
unless it really matters and then not to seek
personal gain, but for the good of all concerned;

having given it, one's word cannot be spurned
due to circumstance or personal cost,
otherwise human relationship is lost
because there is no trust; our word
is tossed onto the wind like a frail bird
caught in a fierce storm.
It does unspeakable harm.

His Garment Is Covered With Dust
(Tagore)

I went to the temple but
You were not home Beloved;
I read the sacred books
but could not hear Your voice;
I chanted the mantras, sang
all the lovely songs, sat
in silent meditation, prayed, fasted,
carried water for the Master,
still I could not find You
anywhere.
Then I went alone into the forest,

sat on a boulder by the river,
watched the Sun travel
among the leaves, and
I heard You breathing in the trees,
Your breath cooled my fever,
stilled the asylum of the mind,
slowed everything down.
When I went to work for the carpenters,
carrying tin to the roof, nailing tar paper,
gluing window flashing, bending in the dust
to clean up scraps, there, Oh there

You were at last my Sweet Lord, there
in the dust, Your robes of light soiled,
dirty, dust covered, only there where the mind
never thought to look did You reveal Yourself.
Sly One, clever beggar, mischievous child,
You baffle the mind oh cunning One, You

(continues)

hide in plain sight where it cannot see You,
You cover Yourself with dust and clothe Yourself
in beggar's rags so it sneers its way past You,
lifting its eyes to heaven and
beseeching the wind.

Yogi Ramsuratkumar

Some say He is on a level with Jesus Christ but
they don't say that in the town where I live or else
they would be murdered and

you couldn't find a jury in 7 counties
that would convict. But you get the idea,
He is something unusual in a world

where we pay snot-nosed boys millions
to hit a ball and they complain in public
about how badly they are treated.

Yogi Ramsuratkumar's body is eaten up
with cancer and though I have never seen Him
I am told His face remains radiant despite

the horror of the bodily pain, but one day
they carried Him out in a stretcher and
placed Him before the crowds and He said,

This Beggar cannot help today, He is
in too much pain, and so they carried Him off
where it was said that they could hear Him

crying out with the pain; still, those who
worshipped Him never stopped whining and complaining
and making demands upon Him, grasping, sucking,

never ceasing no matter how terrible His suffering and
I guess in that way you could make a case
for His being very much like Jesus and

(continues with stanza break)

no jury would deny you that, even
as they sentenced you to
life on Earth without parole.

Yogi Ramsuratkumar: Our Father

His consciousness is like our Sun's, which is
the Masculine Principle in our system,
the Good Father; He shines on all equally,
the good, the bad, the twisted and lame
impartially, impersonally; He is
reliable and consistent, ever-present,
tireless, working for the good of all,
sacrificing His life unconditionally
so that others may live;
He is the life-giver, the Saviour,
the center around which we revolve,
the Star which creates a world and
helps it to thrive, the representative
of Our Creator in the local universe;
He is Non-Judgmental Love,
patient and kind; He is the Sun and
we are the Moon reflecting His Glory;
Hallowed is His Name, His Will
is done on Earth as it is in Heaven,
He forgives all and delivers us from evil,
He gives us each day our sustenance,
He never fails; He is
the Good Father.

The Death of Yogi Ramsuratkumar

When the King of the World dies there is the greatest joy
and a thankful weeping in the streets of Heaven.
Mister Death, your fair-haired boy
has taken all that you and your kind have given

and come out covered in roses;
now He dances in the mourning flames,
His petal-strewn body is given over to the mortal poses
of the burning ghat, but Death has no claims

on the Soul of Yogi Ramsuratkumar, King
of the World. He has a Lawful ticket out of this place,
having found a successor who will wear His ring
and bear the world's agony with a smile on His face.

Mister Lee, Son of the World King, we who adore You
tremble at what is asked of us and bow down before You.

How A Master Dies

I want to tell you the most astonishing thing,
how a Master dies.
3 years ago Mister Lee was diagnosed
with throat cancer; He requested
that we not speak of it. He suggested
that we guard our thoughts since most
of us are addicted to fear and a wise
man knows thoughts are like leeches, they cling

to a person and suck his blood dry. A king
may command, but He begged us to awaken, His cries
a hoarse whisper, then a faint plea, like a ghost
trying to speak through a veil. The Master of infinite jest,
He joked and cursed and shocked and Blessed
us, worked without ceasing, held His post
in His Father's Work to the very end. I tell you no lies:
without complaint or self pity, He endured terrible suffering

for our benefit, that we might rejoice and embrace
our own death with poise, a soft smile on our face,
or raging in a furious noise, working tirelessly in a race
with death, but always loving God, the only Grace.

The Death of A Conscious Man
(Mister Lee)

i.
His beauty is infused in the world,
the sea heaves,
there is a trembling in the leaves,
all the banners of the grasses unfurl.
Adore. Adore.

There are only dry eyes at our table;
we laugh at death's feeble efforts
to claim what it is unable to seize,
what slips its grasp with ease.

He never repeats Himself.
He flies south to His Father, a sweet
soft song on His lips;
He cheats death and yet

His humility is endless.
If you see a new star in the night sky
where none ever was before,
it is my Master.
Adore. Adore.

ii.
We tie our women to the bedpost
or they would throw themselves
naked into the burning sky, nipples straining,
yearning to be nearer to the Holy Ghost.
Adore. Adore.

His absence fills the space, stuns every room
into silence, moves like a bad dream
through a troubled sleep. Nothing is as it seems,
everyone is broken by the impending doom

of the torn and ravaged flesh and bone.
I am an old man alone, deafened
by the silence which remains
after you have left this world bereft.

Though you are gone, you alone remain;
the joy of the wind sings your pure delight.
Happiness is all you want from us;
what else are we here for?
Adore. Adore.

My Master's Body Dead In the Darshan Hall

I come before Your body lying in state
as a leper dragging his stumps comes
before the gates of the city, a bell
clangoring around his neck
to warn off the populace.
What kind of love can a broken
and ruined man like me possibly lay
before the feet of the King of Heaven?
I take the love You have offered me,
the multitude of miracles, the showering
of the flowers of plenitude at my feet;
I take all You have offered as a child
takes without question the generosity
of his mother's breast.
Perhaps that simplitude, the leprous beggar
gratefully receiving proffered alms, that
humble accepting of Your gifts,
is itself an act of love and
all the love I have ever been able
to give. Perhaps
such a poverty of feeling
is enough to please Your noble heart.
The leper tears off his rags
and covers the body of the fallen Christ.

The Ascension of Our Lord In Multi-Colored Robes

Friends, I have seen great wonders:
each of my daughters' heads crowning
at their births as the Divine
entered headfirst into this world;
2 red-tailed hawks flying directly
into the Sun on the 4th day
of my fasting and prayer vigil;
one time I ran out of gas
just in front of a gas station.

But on the day of Mister Lee's Mahasamadhi
2 rainbows appeared,
one end of their arc touching down
in the valley just where His Stupa stood, and
the rainbows persisted for most of the day
until the burial ceremony was finished.

Make what you will of this fact, but
in the real world this was Grace and Mercy,
not subject to words or thought,
the Will of Our Creator manifesting
as Objective phenomenon.

Mister Lee hid His great mastery
artfully, cloaking it in beggar's rags, but
at His death, His Majesty and Radiance
stood fully revealed, Lord of the Universe
clothed in a Baul's multi-colored robes of Light.

Mystical Grace

There is such a thing as Mystical Grace,
we all know that,
when a grand thing happens that
you didn't deserve or earn, but
are momentarily humbled and grateful.

But that doesn't explain Mister Lee's
departure from this world, or at least
from this body.
The Shamanic tradition describes a thing
which they call the Rainbow Body.
It works like this:

when a Being has gathered enough
inner force of Attention, there is created
within, a fully articulated energy body
which Shamans call the Rainbow Body, which
comes about from Conscious labor,

intentional suffering, and
the dissolution of self importance,
no desire. Mister Lee's departure was marked
by the appearance of a double rainbow
which is extraordinary, even in the Shamanic
tradition. It marks the passing

of a truly great Shaman, one
with impeccable Intent
and enormous Will of Attention.
In some traditions such a display
is called Mystical Grace.

Be Not Far From Me

The only happiness is loving You,
its loss the only sorrow.
In death we did not lose You; Your love
rains down upon us, the wind is your breath,
it blows the flowers from Your tomb;
You ring the Sun in light, You
invert the rainbow to smile upon us.
Your love has conquered death in such a way
that the blind can see, the fool
lifts up his eyes before Your Glory,
the madman lays down his sorrows,
the lame and halt rise up and dance,
the lost and wretched are made whole.
Be not far from me my sweet Mother Guru,
come to me on the dusty trail, come
in the troubled sleep, yea come
though I stray, come after me and
accompany me in the Valley of Death.
Your love binds me to You as the Earth
and Sun are bound to the Heavens, the sea
to the embrace of the shore.
You are never further from me
than my next breath,
as day follows night, as the shadow
follows the oxcart over the field.
Oh be not far from me my Beloved
for my heart breaks with such tenderness that
my soul is branded with Your name eternally;
I am lost in You, I am found by You,
I will dwell in Your house forever.

Be A Disgrace

(Rumi)

Mister Lee is a complete disgrace,
cracking wise and telling dirty jokes,
profaning every holy place,

acting and dressing like plain folks,
the hidden Yogi, Lord of the Universe.
He breaks our hearts like egg yolks

and throws us in the frying pan, or worse
directly into the blazing fire.
He steals every coin from our purse,

leaves us with a begging bowl full of desire
for God and then He disappears.
That dirty beggar, that filthy liar,

He promised us God and gave us our fears
instead, made us look at them, stand
before them without lying for years

while He played in a blues band
and ran through our fingers like sand.
A Guru in heaven is worth 2 in the hand.

Tomfoolery

The Holy Fool is dead,
I have seen His head
carried in on a bronze platter;
it does not matter.

When a Holy Fool dies,
the cries of joy arise in every stone,
the leaves dance alone in a tremble of wind,
and all we who have sinned atone

by laughing brazenly in the face of Death.
Is this the best you have to show me
Mister Death? You don't know me
and you don't own me; every breath

belongs to my Master and He is the Fool
who cheated you in a single roll:
He put all his coins in a Beggar's bowl
and sold His Soul to a Dirty Sinner

who eats you as a snack before dinner.
When a Holy Fool dies, the wolves cry out to the Moon
and the dish lies naked, coupling with the spoon,
the lean are plumped, the fat grow thinner,

and the pundit becomes a mere beginner.
Oh how they dance in the alleys of Hell
when a Fool is saved by a dirty Sinner:
the seas quiet, the trees riot, all is well.

(continues with stanza break)

The Fool bares His ass before a crowd;
He curses baldly and laughs out loud
in every Holy place.
Then He is gone; He leaves no trace,

like the wind coming through an open window:
you cannot catch hold of it, you know it
by the flutter of the curtain;
only then can you be certain.

The Solitary Bird
(for Mister Lee)

What profits a man if he makes great art
and has not mastered himself?
If every wayward thought commands his heart
he is a mere trinket on a pauper's shelf.

What matter if the world bows down before him
if he is not lord of his own emotions;
he is a slave though the world adore him,
a beggar though he rules the oceans.

The man who is the master of his moods,
he alone is able to stand by his word;
his face belongs to him, not to his attitudes.
Though many admire him, he is a solitary bird

who flies always to the highest peak.
He keeps his own counsel, when all about him speak.

How Shall I Address You, Mister Death?

How shall I now address you, Mister Death?
Your Majesty? You're king of this poor state,
the sovereign ruler of the fleeting breath,
the arbiter of every human fate;

perhaps you would prefer we say My Lord,
for you are the undisputed master
of life, the one who has the final word
on timing and degree of each disaster;

yet calling you Your Honor suits you well,
since you judge every living thing at last
and none escape the tolling of your bell,
we all are weighed and measured in your grasp;

still, calling you a dirt farmer seems just:
your minions become dirt, you rule the dust.

Part ii:

The Winnowing Process

The Winnowing Process

The conditions for admission to Pythagoras's School were
that each candidate must undergo 3 years of close observation
of his tone of voice and his laughter, the shape of his body,
the quality of his relationship to family and friends,
especially his parents, and how he spent his leisure time.

If he overcame this initial trial, he was required
to undergo 5 years of silence. Pythagoras explained
that mastery of one's tongue was the greatest challenge.
If at any time he was found wanting in any area,
he was sent away from the School forever.

Upon leaving, he was given a sum equal to
twice the amount he had donated to the School and
a monument was erected in his memory
as if he were dead.
If anyone from the School then met him on the street

he was to be treated as a stranger. This is known as
the Winnowing Process, separating wheat from chaff.
My own Master uses a similar process, equally reliable.
By the use of seemingly erratic and bizarre behavior,
Mister Lee drives off those whose commitment

to His School is weak. Then there is the Sacred Bazaar,
in which he enacts the seamless appearance
of a Jewish merchant,
shamelessly haranguing His disciples to buy more,
exhorting His people to go ever deeper into debt.

(continues with stanza break)

One by one, or in small groups, people are constantly leaving the School.
In this way, those who remain grow reliable, able to endure difficulties without complaint.
This is mastery of one's tongue.

The Abbot

I asked Mister Lee to give me shelter
because I had no hope, going nowhere,
years of work, no change. He said, Yes,
and then He went to work on me. Once

I worked in a slaughterhouse, me and
another guy lifting the skinned meat out of
the skinning vats onto swinging hooks, thick,
heavy work and down at the end of the line

was an old man with blades and saws.
We called him the Abbot like the head
of a monastery because we worked in the
abattoir and he was our holy man;

he sliced and boned the carcass. He was good,
he never wasted a move, he knew just where
the joint was and he went for it every time.
Mister Lee is exactly like that.

He is filleting me, making quick work of it,
no waste, and I take it, I watch it all
come off until the bone is exposed and
the old man lays down his blade,

he walks out onto the loading dock,
he lights one up and smokes it,
waits for the next side of meat
to swing down on its hook.

The Guru Is the Slaughterhouse of Love
(after Rumi)

It's our desire that makes us unfit to eat,
it corrupts the flesh and makes for rotten meat.
We hide from death and so we miss our life,
the way a cheating husband misses a good wife.
With his thumb the butcher makes the scales cheat
but he is impoverished by his own deceit
because he will not fall beneath the Guru's knife
to feed our Lord and end the inner strife;
that dying sends our demons in retreat,
guts and cleans them, ends in their defeat.

The Guru takes the best cuts for Himself,
leaves all the rest to rot upon the shelf.
When yearning for the Guru is our only thrill,
we earn the gift of being killed for Love.

What Obedience To the Guru Looks Like

If you wonder what makes for greatness in a disciple,
some would argue that it is difficult circumstances
and hard work that create a sense of urgency,
determination, and fierce devotion which result in
what we call greatness. Like Milarepa, or
take John Unitas as an example, a man who was
discouraged from ever playing football, cut

from one team after another, and became finally
as great a quarterback as ever played the game.
Some say his greatness began with the love of his mother.
Just watching how hard my mother had to work
was the greatest thing I ever saw, he once said.
He told the story about coming home late one day,
exhausted from a long and bruising football scrimmage.

His mother met him at the door;
she ran the family's coal delivery business.
Mrs. Wrigley up the street has 3 tons of coal
sitting in her yard. Go shovel it in her cellar,
she ordered young John.
When he protested that it was raining, she said,
Yes it's raining. Go do it.

And he did, without another word.

Angel of Mercy

Help me Master, the levee has broken
and I've nowhere else to go but You.
Help me. These are the truest words I've spoken;
if there's no room in Your boat, I'm through,

it's over, the flood waters will cover me.
My house is floating downstream
and I don't know what's come over me,
every prayer I offer is a scream:

Help me Master! Mind can't understand,
the levee's broken and there's no dry land,
the gators and the snakes are close at hand
and nothing's going the way I'd planned.

Help me Master, that's my only prayer;
it is on every breath,
my heart is broken, I am ruined, stripped bare
and the only friend I have save You is Death,

so help me please, I know who You are.
You're the Angel of Mercy and You've come like fire
to light the way through darkness, a burning star;
I sing your praises like a broken, ruined choir.

All my levees were built on sand,
they gave way in the high wind and
rising tide. Desperate times demand
desperate measures; help me or I am damned.

The Bardo of Loneliness

Beloved I am so far from you just now,
lost in the bardo of loneliness,
which does not allow You to enter;

they lock the gates when You come and
Oh my Dearest without You it is
so unspeakable a madness. There is laughter

all around but no joy in it. They pour the wine,
set out the food, light the pipe, but nothing
satisfies.

Without You, the leaves grow yellow and fall
and the birds no longer sing, their call
such a far off echo in the empty sky.

Oh my Beloved can You hear my broken cry
here in the poisoned, ruined garden?
Where is Your touch in my hardened heart, where

oh where is Your sweet voice? Come to me Dearest
that I may rejoice; come to me and lead me from
these streets of sorrow to where there is no tomorrow,

into Your quiet temple. No more the loud denial,
no more the turning from Your smile and the light
of Your eyes. All that lives here moves

but does not shine.

Madness Cannot Stand My Master's Face

Master, You have completely undone me,
torn me from my comfort zone of dreaming
and pretending, lying and constant scheming;
all the old tired tricks that used to run me

lost their charm
once I saw the honesty of Your simple Grace.
Dear Master, I suffer to look into Your face
because I see reflected there the harm

I do to self and others by my selfish lazy
ways; though they still have power to seduce,
I can no longer use ignorance as my excuse
for being crazy.

Serving You, I can't dance to the same old tune;
better to try emptying the ocean with a spoon.

One-Trick Pony

We are sipping tea and he asks me,
Do you ever write anything besides poetry?
No, I tell him; I'm not smart enough

to do 2 things at once. In this lifetime,
which is very brief, I want to do
one thing well, to master one thing

rather than do several things half-assed.
So I labor with the poems, praying
for help, thrilled when occasionally one of them

comes out right. Tina Zuccarello built an
entire Ashram with just a backhoe, nothing more.
It is the same with the Dharma practices;

I concentrate on self observation, praying
to get one thing right, to ride that horse
all the way to the river's edge before

I dismount and get in the boat.
One single thing in a lifetime done well
is more pleasing to the Guru

than ten thousand good intentions;
one thing
done well is the only beauty there is.

Thy Sea Is So Great And My Boat So Small
(for Mister Lee)

I have been at sea a long time and
the wind has not always been in my favor:
I have often set sail at the wrong time and
like a man with a high fever

I have steered an erratic course.
Somehow, and it is by Your Grace alone,
I have not floundered on the rocks, or worse
gone down with all hands, our fate unknown.

I sail such a frail, unstable boat
and my hand is unsteady on the helm;
the sea is rough and it is hard to stay afloat.
At every moment I am nearly overwhelmed.

Bless the Pilot who steers through storm-tossed seas,
while on the bridge I tremble on my knees.

A Vigilant Man Guards His Home

The body is our home, but we spend our whole lives
in slavery to it, laboring long hours at work
we mostly hate, for what? To feed, clothe,
and shelter the body. We spend our life force,
that precious breath, on a mind which gives
itself to desire and goes mad, utterly berserk
with an unending thirst for more, and is loathe
to yield to the smallest discipline, like a Horse

who has taken the bit and run over a cliff,
taking us with it to our inevitable doom.
Life lived in insatiable desire is grief,
robs us of dignity, leaves us empty and undone;
a vigilant man guards his home against that thief,
never sleeps, keeps a watchful eye on every room.

The Devil Always Finds Work

The Devil likes chocolate;
that makes it hard not to like the Devil.
God also likes chocolate but
it's easier not to like God because
It only likes chocolate in moderation.
God would never eat the whole box
of chocolates in one sitting, but
that's the only way the Devil does business.
So, no matter how bad the economy,
there could be a worldwide depression,
the Devil always finds work.

We need the Devil;
He takes the blame for everything:
The Devil made me do it; God
never takes the blame, It just forgives
our sins. It's not the same.
I want someone to blame.
With forgiveness comes guilt;
blame feels better.
We have to keep the Devil employed so
when we say,
I can't believe I ate the whole thing,

we know exactly who to blame.

The Lord And Owner of His Face
(Shakespeare: Sonnet 94)

We are a mass of contradictions and of lies,
who cannot help doing what we despise.
Our every move is stolen from our past,
our feet move in the choreography of our vast
inheritance. Yet it is our faces
which most disgrace us,
for they are the masks of our conceit,
hide nothing, reveal our smallest deceit.

But my Master is one who owns His face,
is Lord of His body and moves with conscious Grace.
In Him nothing is out of line;
He reveals what He wishes, otherwise no sign.
He was at Bridge when word came of His dear Master's
    death.
Three no-trump, He said. No sign, no wasted breath.

3 No-Trump

Mister Lee was playing Bridge when
the news came that His Master was dead.
He did not change expression;

3 no-trump, He said.
That was it.
When He got the news that He was

desperately ill, He made the decision:
no chemo,
no radiation,

no surgery.
3 no-trump
all over again.

The Subtle Distinctions of the Master

One night I was Mister Lee's partner at Bridge.
We were doing well and scoring when
we got a hand where Mister Lee

bid 3 no-trump.
The person to my left doubled.
When the bid came back to me I said,

I trust You Mister Lee, and then
I redoubled. He looked straight at me.
Know when to trust me,

He said and
we went down three. The Guru is
the only thing in this world that can be trusted;

my trust in Him should be absolute but
that does not free me from discrimination,
especially when He overbids His hand.

He Left Me In 4 No-Trump

I am playing Bridge with the Guru
who is my partner.
Playing Bridge with the Guru
is an enormous energetic hit,
a direct bodily transmission of finer energy,
a karmic payoff.

I am dealt a big hand;
I bid, He responds,
I go to 4 no-trump,
a slam convention, asking for aces;
it demands that my partner respond.
He passes.

We are doubled, down 3, vulnerable.
Do not ask why He did it, it is irrelevant,
He has His reasons. The Guru is
the incomparable Son of God, the Light
of the world, the Dharma incarnate,
the Lord of the Universe, but

we could have made 6 diamonds.

If You Want To Sit Where I'm Sitting

A group of students is traveling with Mister Lee in India
when He decides to stop for breakfast.
They crowd into the small Indian restaurant and
Mister Lee follows His instincts to some corner tables.
It is hot and crowded so one of His students suggests

they could be more comfortable in a private room in back.
Mister Lee accommodates and everyone moves to the back.
The back room is air conditioned and it is on high.
Soon everyone is cold.
One of the children asks Mister Lee

how she can stop making bad choices and He says,
Learn the difference between instinct and imagination.
How? the child asks. Experience, He replies, and it takes
a very long time. Then
one of His students complains about the cold and

how they would have been more comfortable
at the first table He chose. He is in
an impossible position, everyone
with her own desires, complaints, and ideas about
how it ought to be, totally disrupting the flow of His instinct.

He turns to speak and His eyes are ablaze, His voice fierce:
If you want to sit with me,
you have to sit where I'm sitting.
The difference between instinct and imagination is
knowing when to speak and

when to keep your mouth shut.

Making Conversation With the Master

One evening in the Tavern of the Ruined
I was invited to sit in the company of the Master.
Sometimes I am steady and focused in that company,
sometimes not; that night
not.

So I decide I will make polite conversation.
After 20 years in the Work, this decision should
trigger flashing red lights, alarm bells,
clowns piling out of a little bitty car and
Elephants taking a dump in the center ring but
No;

I say, D. tells me we have sold 1,500 copies
of my book. That means you haven't lost money
on it, I say proudly. We are proud to represent you,
is all the Master says and I think nothing else of it.
The next day, not weeks or months later, but
the next morning, D. comes up to me and says,

Mister Lee has decided to remainder your book.
Now the bells and whistles go off, the dog and pony show
begins and I am the midget in the spotlight
in center ring desperately dodging the Elephant dung.
So after 20 years in the Work I can tell you this much:

when the urge to make polite conversation
with the Master comes upon you,
do not walk, run like your ass is on fire
for the nearest exit before
the Elephant enters the center ring.

Keeping Mister Lee Awake

At midnight, when His band has finished playing,
He has given everything on stage and
I have given everything on the dance floor and
we are both exhausted but

we still have a 2 hour drive to home.
I first notice it 15 minutes onto the road:
He is at the wheel, everyone is asleep and
the van is weaving from side to side in its lane.

I reach over and touch His arm.
Are you okay? I ask.
Yes, He says and that is when I realize
I may be of use to the Master,

I can help Him stay awake, but
I don't want to engage in useless chatter;
I do not want to cross the line
between help and interference so

that is my struggle;
His is to stay awake.
Though we weave now and then
He is able to catch it and come back

without me saying or doing anything.
In some way the quality of my Attention
may help Him. I don't know. Then
20 minutes later we are

headed straight into a concrete wall
before an overpass.   (continues)

At the last possible moment before we die,
I grab the wheel and say, Watch it.

Those 2 times were all that was needed.
Accelerator to the floor, we roared past semis,
sometimes weaving dangerously but

just in time catching it and going straight.

I sat there, relaxed and terrified,
left arm on the arm rest ready to act
but it was never needed again.
He had His struggle and I had mine.

The line between help and interference is rarely spoken
it is so delicate, like the petals of a Lotus:
too much pressure and something beautiful is broken;
done right, its fragrance lingers, nearly escapes notice.

This Path Is the Dirt Road
(for Mister E.J. Gold)

If you come to the Master's School to learn,
you will come away with nothing,
available help will remain hidden from you
and you will wither and fall away.

If you come to the School to work, to
assist in the Master's business, you will
in the course of this work learn some things,
perhaps flourish on the vine and even blossom.

Mister Lee once described those who come
only to learn and not to Work; He said they
fail to practice,
think they are spiritual students yet

cater to the animal's every demand for comfort,
whine and complain,
are oblivious to School protocol and principles,
refuse to sacrifice petty desires

to build Work energy,
think they are spiritual warriors. HA!
He said, standing in the rain and mud of India,
bus exhaust pouring in the windows, students

choking and gagging around Him. HA!
He said, and those who came to learn were
blinded by their own misery;
those who came to Work,

(continues with stanza break)

Worked in the dirt and the filth because
that is where the Work is.
In order to find gold,
you have to get dirty.

Why I Don't Have To Act Crazy Anymore

It got me a long way in life, the crazy routine.
It got me the attention I craved and it kept people
at arm's length which is the way I liked it.
Then I met Mister Lee who is
a lot crazier than I ever had the nerve to be

and a Wise Master as well. One day
Mister Lee was sitting in a café eating
chocolate cream pie.
One of His close female disciples,
thinking she was His familiar,

criticized Him for His manners.
He took the chocolate cream pie and
smashed it on top of His head, fudge and
whipped cream running slowly down His face.
His disciples sat there horrified,

not so much because every single eye in the place
was on the Master's chocolate face,
but because they suddenly understood
in a way they never had before, the line
between respect and familiarity.

It is that kind of Crazy Wisdom
which got me
to come off my act.
I'd rather eat my pie
than wear it.

My Master Touched My Face

One night I am waiting tables at a feast
and Mister Lee is at the head table.
It is a crowded room and someone asks me
to hand out the dessert forks.
I start at the head table and I bend over,
placing forks carefully by each person's place.

Mister Lee stops me and He
says to me, Just ask them
if they want a fork, it's not
so awkward. And then
right there in front of everyone He
reaches up with both hands and smiling,
He holds my face with a look of such
tenderness
that it breaks my heart.

Once Mister Gurdjieff watched as 4 of His
strongest men worked with heavy sledges
to break up a boulder, smashing and smashing but
only every now and then getting a chip.
Mister Gurdjieff stood there for a while, then
He took a small hammer and walked round
and round the boulder, stepped up to it and

tapped, tapped, then with a single swing He
split the stone in 2.
It is not the size of the hammer
but the perfect placement
of the blow.

The Master's Kind Regard

It goes like this, I'm told:
the Master dies and then assumes
any available form so He might
aid His grieving disciple, who pales

in the gloom and grows first sick, then old.
I am under an Oak tree, a rose bush blooms
next to me, and I hear a buzzing as night
gathers around me like canvas sails

gathering the wind. A dragon fly lands, folds
its wings on my shoulder, then zooms
off into the fading light.
The Master's kind Regard never fails.

Respecting the Guru's Domain

There is a sense in which the Guru is owned
body and Soul by His devotees, a sense
in which He is their slave. Ultimately
however, He is the only one among us
who is truly free.

So it shocked and hurt me for Him
when one day I walked into the Guru's
Ashram office where He was set up behind
a table filled with Sacred bronze artifacts,
and I asked if I could speak with Him.

Of course, He said, so I asked if I could
step around the table and enter the small
cramped space where He was sitting.
No, He said and then he looked
straight at me.

Thank you for asking, He said. In all the years
I have sat in this space, you are the first person
who has ever asked me;
the only one.
Write a poem about that, He said, so

that is what I am doing because
there is so little
that can be done
to ease the suffering
of a truly free man.

The Fast Track to Heaven

I'm tired of God;
I'll take Mister Lee any day.
He likes chocolate and good wine
and good looking women. Anyway,
God is a good Guy to have on your side
in a fight but it's better to dine
with Mister Lee who puts out a fine spread.
Thank God for giving us our daily bread,
and Mister Lee for the butter and marmalade,

especially the butter; Mister Lee likes butter.
It's true that Jesus walked on the water
and then He turned it to wine, but even better
than that, Mister Lee turned a damn fool
like me into a reliable and useful tool
to use in His Work; anyone can walk
on water, I've seen ducks do it 100 times,
but who else could transform an idiot to talk
wisely on the Dharma and make rhymes
to praise his Master?
God saves, but Mister Lee's faster.

Making My Master Proud

My Master is an arrogant man, independent
and stubborn, He says so Himself, but
He is also obedient.
I am weak and ignorant, but
when my Master told me,
Sell more books,
I decided that this was a request
that I could obey, even though
I did not like selling the poetry books
because I was shy and ashamed, fearing rejection.

So I sell the books, everywhere I go,
sometimes only one, sometimes
20 or more, and I do it
shamelessly because
that is the way my Master does it.

One time I gave a reading at the Marsh Theatre
in San Francisco before 50 or so people.
I told a joke or 2 and pitched the books.
Afterward a woman came up to buy a book
and laughed. That
was the most shameless hucksterism
I have ever heard, she said
and this made me very happy.
My Master would have been proud.

Every Day With the Guru Is A Good Day

Happiness is a mysterious Stranger,
one of the messengers of God.
You cannot force him, though you seek him
everywhere, but when you least expect it
there he is, like a brief glimpse of the Beloved
across a crowded room.

This morning I stood in the Ashram kitchen
doing dishes with Dasya and we laughed
as we worked in the Guru's Grace.
He teaches us how to live and work together,
what it is to be human and
how to forgive our flaws with laughter.

Many are troubled in the Guru's company
but I am troubled in my own.
Though I am not much good at loving,
am a man of little faith,
I try to do as I am told and when I do,
the Stranger arrives unbidden at my door.

He comes unbidden to the butcher,
muscled arms awash in blood;
he surprises the widow dozing in her
dead husband's chair; he comes
to the man with the rope around his neck
just before they throw the trapdoor handle.

He comes, He comes as the Guru, a rogue upstart
in a thin disguise. Oh my Beloved, my sweet,
I have found your abode in the cave of the heart

(continues)

and though I have crumbs for bread, am able
to serve only scraps for meat,
still you sit down at my table

and you eat.

The Fine Print In the Bodhisattva Vow

Where is it written that you will never retire,
even when you die? In the Bodhisattva contract,
that's where. But it is written in print so fine

that only the stars and galaxies can read it,
and all the Saints smile, break down in
helpless laughter, pound one another on the back,

and howl until their teeth fall out and
they have yet another heart attack in yet another
lifetime of being the joke, when the novice

leans over to sign the contract and asks
in complete innocence, without irony,
What's so funny?

The contract says, You do this work
until you die;
the fine print says,

You never die.

I Loathe In the Morning What I love At Night

In me 2 opposing natures reside,
2 forces at odds, like 2 horses
pulling end to end instead of side by side.
Thus, I can't know what my course is
whenever I set sail;
what draws me towards one shore at night
by morning's light looks worn and pale;
the left hand does not know the right.
That in me which loves Our Lord
is seldom in command,
and when it is I can't afford
thoughtless words, or where I stand
turns quick to shifting sand,
every word or deed exacts a cost,
one careless thought or move and I am lost.

The Blind Spot

We come into this world with a blind spot
around which our entire psychology is constructed,
like a pearl around a single grain of sand.
The function of the psychology is to maintain
the blind spot in a stable position of control;
we become our blind spot.

Everything we do reinforces
the primacy and truth of the blind spot and
we do not see what our blind spot is,
of course, that is why it's called the blind spot.
It is the blind spot which thinks in us,
so you cannot think about it because

it is the thinking mechanism; likewise
our emotional reactions to life are constructed to
reinforce and habitually act out our blind spot.
The Gospel of the disciple Thomas
tells us Jesus instructed His disciples thusly;
Easier to see a mote in your neighbor's eye

than a beam in your own. We can see
the other's blind spot, but not our own,
that is the Law.
The Guru's job, by subtle and skillful means,
is to reveal to us our blind spot, to nail
our foot to the floor so we cannot turn away.

You may laugh at the idea of a Guru and
scoff at those who seek one:
who laughs, and why?

The Disintegration of the Syntax

We have 2 minds, which gives us 2 ways
of perceiving reality. The still mind is never
born, never dies, but is connected directly to reality,
perceives energy directly without interpretation.

The 2nd mind is a chattering mind which holds
the syntax of the culture we are raised in and
filters the energy of reality through this syntax;
this mind is insistent, so sooner or later

it isolates us from reality and dominates our attention.

The function of the guru is to place us in circumstances
which dissolve the syntax of the chattering mind
slowly, a little at a time, until eventually all that is left
is the still mind.

Mister Lee is the Spiritual Master, the Shaman of our lineage
and He is doing this work with me, disintegrating the syntax;
the syntax does not work with Him. Every time that I use it
to approach Him, He freezes me out.

He refuses to be contaminated with my shit.
One day I approached Him and asked if we could talk.
Later, He said.
At the end of that day He called me over.

Now would be a good time, He said; Is this
personal? No, I said.
Thank God, He said and we both laughed
and laughed. He gets it all the time and

it is a relief when anyone is willing to do the work

to shovel and muck the stalls of their own mind,
so He does not have to stand there knee-deep
in their syntax and look at
one more horse's ass.

Shifting the Assemblage Point

A Nagual is a shaman whose energetic configuration
gives Him the power to take responsibility for the fates of
    those
who make up His company of apprentices. Such a Nagual
is Mister Lee, one whose personal power is such that He is
    able
to guide the fates of 100 or so apprentices, often from
great distances and with subtle moves and magical passes
    which
He is an artist of the greatest skill at hiding and
camouflaging under the guise of ordinary activities such as
playing Bridge.

In order to accomplish a very difficult maneuver with me,
shifting my inner center of gravity to save my life, He used the
    Bridge table
as His medium. On 3 separate occasions over a 12 day period
He maneuvered me around the Bridge table so that once I sat
opposite Him as His partner, and twice right next to Him,
    observing
His play of the hands.
On the fourth occasion He placed me with 2 of His most
    accomplished
clowns to lighten my inner mood, which is always overly
    serious and
self important.

Once He had prepared my inner world to accommodate the
    move,
on the 9th day He maneuvered me through His Tavern space
    and

when I failed to hear His invitation to join Him, in one brief
sentence,

Red Hawk is lost in contemplation,
He shifted my center of gravity from the head to the body, as
neat and
efficient a magical pass as I have ever seen; He accomplished
with
as little show and as few words, with a minimum of effort and
subtlety,
as difficult a rearrangement of the inner structure as I could
possibly
imagine, one which I will be years integrating and my body
has still not

recovered from, but has undergone a fierce and difficult inner
purging of
accumulated emotional poisons. His final move, to fix the
assemblage point
in its new position, was on the 12th day, very early in the
morning before Sunrise;
it was so elegant and effective in its simplicity that I will never
forget it:
I stood before Him in bare feet, seeing Him off on his 4
month trip to France.
As He passed me I said, God Bless you Sir, and in one quick
move He
flashed His gaze into my eyes and briefly touched my arm
with His hand,
relocating my center of gravity from head to heart. This is why
Mister Lee

(continues)

is the Nagual of our company,
responsible for the fates of His party of apprentices.
He wastes no motion,
makes only the necessary effort,
no more nor less,
gets the job done
without pretense or show,
impersonally, objectively, cleverly disguised
so as not to call undue attention to Himself.

He is the unknown force in the known habit,
The Magician who pulled this rabbit out of the Devil's hat.

He's All Business

The Guru sits up front on a platform
in a wide chair which is not *like* a throne,
it *is* a throne and

we go up and bow before Him,
bringing gifts like fruit and poems and
we leave them there at His feet but

that is not nearly enough,
He wants more; Give me
all your money, He says so

we buy everything He sells: books and tapes and
more bronze deity statues from India
than you can possibly imagine, tons of bronze,

boatloads, whole continents of bronze but
that is not nearly enough, He
wants more; Give me your obedience,

He says and many fall by the wayside
at this request; money is one thing but this
is different and still we give until it hurts,

though for most the very thought hurts,
and then He saves the best for last because
it is the hardest, nearly impossible: Give me

your suffering, He says and they leave
in droves, the roads leading to hell
are bumper-to-bumper day and night.

(continues with stanza break)

Give me all you've got, everything,
He says, a big smile on His face, and
I'll see what I can do for you;

I know some people in High places.

The End of Slave Days

Half-a-lifetime I have observed
the hold which thought has on me;
like a cowed slave shackled
to his master, I did as I was told;
I believed in thought.

All random thoughts,
without a Conscious Watchman,
are liars; all they desire is illusion,
a man on a wild Horse
trying to rope a shadow.

He who stays quiet,
inside the moment, watches
every vagrant impulse to think arise, and
stays with his breath instead, unshackled
from the illusory chains which bound him.

If you chain the leg of a baby Elephant
to a stake, then when he is grown you may
bind him with a thread and he will
remain forever bound. He is like a man
who does not watch his thoughts.

And Always Comes the Dark Before the Dawn

You brought 22 of us to Boulder,
spread fire over the mountain and
drove the Buddhists down into our arms;
they Blessed us, and we them.
Then You brought the rain to ease the fire,
showered Your Love upon us so that
You left me with little choice but to

open my eyes and see You everywhere
in our midst, speaking in tongues of fire,
baptizing us in rain, thus
a man of little faith like me emerged
with nothing but Faith to guide me
in doing the Work that You have given,
to clothe the ghosts of hell in rags of Heaven.

And always comes the dark before the dawn
when the old ways are set against the new
and You appear to die and now are gone,
yet still there is the glistening morning dew;
Your Grace relieves the scorched and rain-starved lawn.
Does everything in life bow down to You,
including me? I'm Blessed to be Your pawn

and let Our Lord control the playing field;
It rules in Grace, while my place is to yield.
Without defense I stand, nothing concealed;
You are my rod and staff, my lance and shield.

The Angel Is Burning

I see the Angel in me burning, burning,
its Heart is on fire with the Guru.
I try to put out the fire
by any means, but

nothing, nothing
will put out the fire. It is
consuming the Heart.
I do not want this.
I do not know what this is.
I have never seen this before.

Oh my friends, once the Angel
catches fire, it is too late
to beg for Mercy! It is too late
to turn back, it is too late to wish
you had never opened this door.

All you can do is burn and
burn to death, until
there is nothing left of you
but the Guru.

When you hear of Saints being
burned at the stake, the hand gestures
they make through the flames are
instructions to the Angel in us
who burns alone and unseen.

Every Spiritual Path Has A Pathology

Desire is the snake on the path.
Every time there is a breakthrough
on a spiritual path,
desire awaits.
If I succumb to it,
pathological behavior results:
the abuse of power, often sexual,
self importance, self-righteousness,
lying.
No matter how advanced the practitioner,
when this happens
everything is lost,
everything.
It happens at every level of practice,
we are tempted by desire.
When the Gospels say Jesus was
tempted by the Devil,
they mean desire;
it is the only Devil.
All human pathology
arises from it:
when one is without desire,
there is only God.

You Dirty Little Trickster

You dirty little Beggar, You and Your trickery;
I thought once You were dead I was free,
that I could relax and take it easy,
but No. It only made it easier to trick me.
You got me looking one way, then
with the other hand You grabbed me
by the throat and hauled my ass in,
a big fat fish gasping on the bank and
now I know exactly who to thank
for the world of trouble You've got me in.
Why me, Master? Of all people,
why a hopeless little Idiot like me
having to travel the world training people
when I am barely house-trained myself?
Alright, I no longer pee on the dining room floor
or stare at every bum and street corner whore,
but You've got me working with people and
I don't want to do that, it scares me
and it troubles me and it wears me
out. Australia called, then France and I said
No,
because You were dead and I thought
I could get away with it; Boulder called and I fought
it but I saw You were never going to leave me
alone,
never, so I gave up on hiding. There's no place
to hide from You, nowhere to run, no space
that You do not occupy. You tricked me Master, but
the greater miracle is that You tricked Death who
thought He had You in His grasp
once He sucked out Your last gasp

(continues)

but You are still not out of breath. You
just use my breath to speak and that is sneaky
as Heaven You dirty little Trickster You.

The Next New Thing

The hunger never ceases,
it must be fed;
as the size of the belly increases,
so too does the head.
This is how it goes, Master:
a modest success can soon become a disaster
from gossip, one of the new diseases
with which the seekers wish to be infected.
The herd stampedes, the cliff's neglected
and we race mindless to our certain doom.
22 of us were stripped naked in a room
and for 2 days made to stand in fire;
no one in that room could be a liar
but now that we are free, without restraint,
only self control can save us from complaint
or too much praise;
both can feed the herd's fear-driven craze
and headlong rush for the next new thing.
When words are few and actions sing
our praise for us,
only then may we join the Hallelujah Chorus.
Let each become Her Master's humble slave
and then the Hungry Ghosts will cease to rave.

Spiritual Capitalist

He was once beautiful to look at, but
now it is hidden by the ravages
of cancer, his, and suicide, his wife's.
He has been torn to pieces by life and
he has fallen into the common trap
of trying to understand the Why of things
when it is impossible to understand, we
are not made in such a way that
we can understand; it is a profound drain
on available energy. He searches desperately
for answers where there are none,
endlessly repeating the details of her tragedy
to anyone who will listen; that number
grows increasingly smaller. No one
can take it for long.

I have settled upon Guru Worship
as the Path for me in this lifetime because
I am a Spiritual Capitalist and
Guru Worship offers the greatest profit
for the energy expended;
it eliminates the futile need to understand.
Once I have found Mother Guru and
am certain of my course, then
all that is required of me is obedience;
Faith follows obedience
as the dog follows a good master.
Obedience is a short leash and
I am the Guru's good dog,
the son of a bitch, who does
as he is told.

Eat the Sun

The Moon devours us.
It is a Lawful process; because the Moon
is of the Earth's body, in the same way

that a newborn devours its mother, the Moon
must feed to grow; exactly as the green shoot
at the growing tip of a branch gathers sap

which is sent down the branch to feed it,
so too the Moon is sent energetic food
from the Earth in order for it to thrive.

Its food is negative emotions
which radiate from the Earth like
a crack whore emanates futility and death.

All war, violence of every kind, physical or
emotional or verbal, from fist or tongue,
feeds the Moon.

The Sun, on the other hand, exists
to be devoured.
It radiates goodness, but only they

whose hearts are opened and surrendered
may receive this goodness, eat it, digest
it, and allow it to pass through them

unimpeded, not squandered and used up
by the million petty dramas of the neurotic mind.
They who eat the Sun are called enlightened and

                              (continues with stanza break)

they are an unselfish light in the sorrows of the world.
They are like old wise men who plant trees
whose shade they know they will never sit under.

Placing Hope In What Is Permanent

Hope in the body is sickness and death;
it weakens as it ages and runs out of breath.

Hope in the mind is denial and madness;
it lies, steals our joy and ends in sadness.

Hope in the emotions is anger and fear;
they fight and flee love, waiting for a savior to appear.

Hope in Conscience is the doorway to the Divine;
not my will be done, but Thine.

Hope in consciousness develops the Soul;
there is no end to Its growth, the path is the goal.

Hope in conscious death leads me to conscious labor:
despite my flaws and his, I work to love my neighbor.

Old Age Requires the Greatest Courage
(for Mister Lee)

The greatest courage is not needed for war,
but for ordinary people growing old.
Like soldiers, the aged are never very far
from death: many are called,
all are chosen. A soldier faces danger
then retreats, but for the old, going back
is not possible; they may hunger
for youth but pray for the luck
of a quick death. When one by one
the body's systems fail, they must be brave
and face annihilation of the flesh and bone,
the Soul clinging like a shipwrecked sailor, to love;
finally, love is all we are given
to navigate between exhaustion and heaven.

The Attainment of High Spiritual Powers

There is an ancient spiritual practice
whose power is attained only by
the highest practitioners, called Tumo Yoga,
the intentional generation of body heat.
The initiate in this practice,
after years of training, is taken
to a frozen lake high in the mountains
in the dead of winter,
stripped naked and
wrapped in frozen blankets
that were soaked in the lake.
Using meditation techniques
learned over many years, he
melts these blankets and dries them
generating Tumo body heat alone.
Personally I have mastered,
over a lifetime of practice,
the even greater Yoga of
throwing another log
on the fire.

Practice of the Dharma

Some men climb the highest mountains
and they endure terrible hardships;
some men go to war where they see
and endure unimaginable suffering;
some men pursue money, sex, power,
fame or drugs and for them there is
no end to the pain and longing of the spirit.

But woe unto him who finds the Dharma
and seeks to Practice what he learns there,
for the suffering he must endure
cannot be spoken; the hardships
he must endure are more terrible than
all others and his spirit will be broken;
he will be left trembling and afraid, naked
as the worst addict, bereft as the poorest beggar,
troubled and shamed as the whoremonger
and the thief.

Do not undertake to Practice the Dharma friend,
I warn you, I implore you, I beg you, for
you will be found out,
your secrets will be exposed as if they were
the common gossip in the bars and alleys
of hell. Everything which you hold dear
will be taken from you and you will be
left weeping and gnashing your teeth,
alone as the day you entered this world and
more naked because even your innocence
will be taken from you and you will be
thrown at the feet of God with nothing,

nothing to clothe you, nothing to sustain you,
nothing but your Practice of the Dharma, and
friend, it will exact from you the last and
most precious coin held tight in your
sweating hand. On this trip a man may
take nothing with him, nothing
will accompany him save his Practice.
The Dharma is a terrible Master; all
who undertake it must die; no one
has ever survived.

So What?

Your dog disappeared and never came back?
So what.
Your neighbor encroached on your property and
refused to correct it?
So what.
Your parents didn't love you?
So what?
You caught your mate in bed with your best friend?
So what.
Your husband died of a heart attack and
you have been told you have 3 weeks to live?
So what.
We are all born to die?
So what.
The human race is on the verge of extinction?
So what.
The atomic bombs are all in the hands of lunatics?
So what.
Everything is what it is,
exactly as it is; all meaning and all suffering
derive from judging it good or bad,
which is arbitrary, subjective, relative and
meaningless.
You completely and vehemently disagree?

So what.

Part iii:

The Sacred Prostitute:
Awakening the Feminine

Submission Is the Secret of Love
(Mister Lee)

Mastery is complete submission.
I knew nothing of this until
my marriage, where
slowly it dawned on me that
worship of the Goddess was
the only hope for peace
in the marriage and
in me. So

that is the practice I undertook.
Oh my friend the secret surprise
which that revealed to me:
the deeper my surrender
to this worship,
the more I was worshipped in return;
the greater my devotion,
the more profound the devotion
which was given to me.

The Way of Submission and Worship
opens to the secret heart of love.
We men are taught to rule,
to demand that others submit, thus
the secret heart remains elusive,
forever beyond our grasp.
We prefer our suffering, but
Divine knowledge comes only
on bended knee.

Only then am I free.

For God So Loved the World He Gave It Whores

You can't keep them down or out,
you can't legislate them out of business,
you can't fence them in and keep them

in one district of your town, you can't
shout or shame or preach them away, they will
still show up in the mayor or the preacher's bed

at the cheap motel on the edge of town.
They are the world's oldest profession because
they are what men want;

oh, they will take wives but
they will pay whores to do for them
what wives cannot even think about;

whores know what men like.
Wives can't even speak of it because
they do not have the tongue to please;

wives can't hear of it because
their orifices are not open to the truth.
If you would please the Guru Lovers,

you must become His whores, they
who will do the unspeakable for Him, who
will perform the unthinkable acts which

cause a Saint's robes to rise in sheer delight.

Don't Come To Me With Your Whining And Complaining

Don't come to me with your whining and complaining, Lovers
because I spit on suffering,
yours and mine as well.

I lay all suffering at my Master's feet,
put kohl-black beneath my eyes,
bejewel my navel, wear hoops at ear

and bracelets at wrist and ankle
so that I may dance and sing
for Him and Him alone.

This suffering does not belong to us Lovers,
it is His gift, it is all such Idiots and
drunken knaves such as we

have to offer a King.
What do you think Lovers,
that you lay virtues before Him?

Don't make me laugh,
I have weak bowels and will soil myself.
What virtues, what conceivable goodness

could miscreants such as we
possibly possess that would interest a Lord?
Don hoop and bracelet Lovers,

dance like sluts before the King of Pimps;
He pimps for the Lord and we are
His harem, His stable, His brothel; we are

the whores by which He lures the coins of Heaven.

No Ordinary Woman

I am no ordinary woman Lovers,
I am the Guru's whore,
all big tits and brazen ass

'cuz that's the way He likes them, full of sass.
These words are my tits,
these poems my big ass shaking

out there in the wind breaking
for all to smell and see, but
for Him alone to fondle and adore.

I am His whore.
You can look all you want Lovers,
but you do not have what it takes

to lay me down. You may see what shakes,
but you will never see my underwear
'cuz I don't wear any;

this big bootalicious fanny
shakes only for Him Lovers.
You get the teases, but

He alone gets what pleases.

How To Attract the Guru

Lovers, if you would attract the Guru's eye
you must become the kind of whore
men slash their canvases for
and smash their bronzes upon the floor,
the kind of whore for whom men die.

You must develop an unquenchable inner fire,
become a nymphomaniac for God, such that mere sight
of you arouses the Guru's inner Light
and creates such hunger in Him that you cannot fight
Him off with an army of mercenaries for hire.

Lovers, do you think me crude
and talk such as this base blasphemy?
Attracting the Guru's gaze requires an inner alchemy;
even to gain entrance into His Academy
requires a radical transformation of mood and attitude.

Do you think yourself above such base displays,
that you would never deign to tear off your skirt
and grovel and roll naked in the dirt,
sacrificing all your precious virtue and comfort
in order to win the Guru's slightest praise?

Well I am exactly that kind of whore, see,
that kind and no other,
the kind who would sell her own mother
into slavery and betray her son and brother
if it would cause the Guru to adore me.

Come To God Dressed For Dancing

My Master sings lead in a bad ass blues band;
He makes the choices very simple, either I come creeping
to God in a funeral procession and
surrounded by lamentations and weeping

or
I come like a whore
on payday, loud and prancing
my stuff, dressed for dancing,

kohl-black under my eyes, bracelets jangling
in a bawdy symphony;
my Master does not ever cry or beg for sympathy
but comes to God braided and tattooed, earring dangling

from one pierced lobe. There is no weeping in His abode;
His God is not a heavy load.

The Smart Whore Goes Where the Money Is

Lovers, I am not one of you.
I am a street whore
who goes with the smart money.

Your Guru is a bronze merchant and
a peddler of religious relics and on the street
He has the reputation of being a King

among the merchants and peddlers,
the one with the touch of gold,
the Midas among Masters.

These poems are oral sex
for the Merchant with the most gold.
Lovers, I am not one of you,

I am the whore with a heart of bronze.

In the Land of the Blind, the One-Eyed Man Is King

Man, thy name is Legion, the Gospels say.
What is meant is simply this:
I am a pimp.
Inside this body you see is another body
made of 100 habits; each habit calls itself
by the same name: I, as in,
I like, I don't like, I want, I don't want, and

I am their pimp;
whatever their wish, I am their boy.
For a hundred lifetimes this legion of I's
has owned me and shaped my destiny.
But in this lifetime
I found the Guru and He is the difference.

Whatever He wishes, I am the Guru's boy.
So dear Master, my Beloved
I come to a Beggar begging:
make me a one-I'd man,
give me an inner unity, make me
master of my domain, such that

I am not carried by every easy breeze,
I do not chase after every pretty whore,
when fear knocks on my door let there be
no one at home and when anger calls for me
in the back alleys and gutters of hell,

let those who dwell there in the burning shame
and the dark sorrows of the night say to him,
he does not live here anymore; he lives
on the hill station with the Beggar, he is
one who has escaped, made his way
over the barbed wire and away from the
eternal burning, he is the dishwasher
in the Guru's kitchen, he

is the busboy at the Guru's table,
he sweeps the stables and
scrubs the Guru's floors, he
does not drink with the pimps or
lay with the whores
anymore.

Master, I beg you.
Let me be your lackey, your bootblack,
the rug upon which you wipe your bare feet,
the rag with which you catch your tears,
the unguent you rub upon your sores,
the pimp who hustles for you
down the avenues of the gods.

The City of the Mind

I have gotten a good look at the alternative city
which my mind builds to reside in, the separate reality
which it proposes for my consideration whose
primary characteristic is the void created
by refusal to love God. The ruler of this dark world

is self-hatred. Whores lounge in every doorway,
hurtful judgments are spat upon passersby,
couples flagellate one another, drawing blood,
crowds delight in public hangings, and
the creator-mind is standing on every corner

clothed in my flesh, shaking its head at me
in disappointment: No good, it says and at last
I am led to wonder, Can the love of God
possibly be any worse than this?
Many are they who question

the Lover of God,
criticizing His deportment,
damning His motives.
In the city of the mind,
every whore has an opinion.

Sacred Dancing

Each morning I sit on the cushion
before the murti of the Master and
I enter into the Sacred Dance
with God, the Blessed coming
and going away;

a thought will arise which
catches Attention and I am lost
into the world of fascination
and desire, like a bad dream; then
the Grace and Mercy of Our Lord,

that sweet call, like a Mother
calling her child to her side,
brings me back to the present where
all Grace and Mercy dwell, the
low hum of the refrigerator like

a Mother's soft lullaby.
This is the dance of desire,
moving away from Mother Guru
into the raging torrent, then
back into the Sacred Heart of Mercy.

Oh, I am become a Momma's Boy
Beloved Master, one who cannot bear
to leave Your Blessed side even for
a moment; the pain is like a child's
orphaned from his Mother. Let me be

(continues with stanza break)

forever tied to Your apron strings Master;
carry me across the river of sleep
in Your sweet arms;
cradle me in Your Heart of Grace;
pray, rock me with Your Name until I wake.

We Speak of Tomorrow

We speak of tomorrow as if
it were real, something certain and
guaranteed, a promise
made by time, a fact
instead of a figure of speech,
a figment
of our imagination, the past
projected into imagination only
now perfected, the errors
of the past sanded down and
hand rubbed until smooth,
no sharp edges, no splinters;
it is how we refuse responsibility
for what is right in front of us, for
the hearts we have broken
which cannot be repaired.

Oh My Lord, Consume Me

Oh my Lord, dear Master, let me drink
from your cup in the Tavern of broken hearts.
I would rather be drunk from your sorrows,
dance to the beat of your tambourine
in the street of broken dreams and turn aside
from the symphony of desire to be the bride
of your wedding chamber,
the unspoiled virgin of the Sacred cloth,
the tremble in your longing, the mote
of the dust of your foot.
Take me dear Lord, lift me up
from the dead where the wind mutters
and groans through the scattered bones
and heal my shattered heart.
You are at last the only thing that matters
when I dance no more with the whores
of thought or slave in the fields of desire.
Consume me in the fire of Your longing,
let me burn with worship, give me
the Grace of Your slavery, erase
me completely so it is Your face alone
that I see in the mirror, Your breath
that remains when death comes for me,
You alone who are left to adore me when I yield,
am stripped of these garments and
my bones are a feast for the beasts of the field.

Prasad

Beloved Master, I lay this body,
this life, at Your Holy feet; this
is the only Prasad I have for You
so I bring it here and lay it

before You, that You and Your Father
may be nourished; this offering
to the Guru is food for His life.
It is a small and poor gift, but

You are able to turn dross to gold,
I have seen it. You have conquered
Death itself and You can make use
of such a humble gift as this life.

Every thought is Your Prasad,
every emotion is Your Prasad,
every breath is Your Prasad Master.
Surrender it in Love;

make me Your food.
Consume me.

I Belong To Mister Lee

I am a single breath in the noseholes
of Mister Lee; it is His music
which comes out of my mouth, His poems
which scratch their way across
the endless paper desert looking
for water.
Did you think you have a life, Lovers?
Is that what you thought, that
this illusion of a life was real and
that it belonged to you?
This belly laugh you hear at such
childish nonsense is Him, roaring
like a Lion in the brush. He is
waiting patiently to devour your life
for His supper; He knows every path
you take to the waterhole and
when He wishes, He will snap you up.
Do you hear that breathing as you
lie there in the dark, dreaming
that you have a life, Lovers?
Did you think that was your breath?
Did you think it was you laughing?

Heart Snatcher

Lovers, beware.
The Guru is a magician beyond compare;
Houdini broke out of locks and chains
but my Master has broken into what remains
of my well-fortified and heavily guarded heart,
has penetrated my defenses and ripped apart
the veil of fear and lies

which makes up my pitiful disguise.
Lovers, the Guru has seen right through my grief
and madness, has stolen my heart like a thief
in the night, and has left me bereft of reason
like a tree which has bloomed out of season,
dropping all of my leaves in the spring,
and in winter birds nest in my limbs and sing.

His Heart Beats Me

Who am I kidding, Lovers?
I am not other than Mother Guru,
He is not different than me, there is
only He whose heart

beats me, the way
a poor woman down by the river
kneels delicately among the stones and
beats her old rags and patched linens

on the river stones to clean them, at least
to remove the dust and loosen the sweat stains
from the warp and woof of the fabric;
just as He beats me

whose heart is soiled with the accumulation
of sorrows, though His beating is subtle
like the woman who drapes her linens and
soft secret silken garments across a line

placed in the Sun, whose steady heat
and brilliant light bleach out all stains so
the garment has a brightness and a sweet
fragrance from the Sun beating upon it.

In this same way Lovers,
His heart beats me, its steady, unceasing
rhythm bleaching out what is soiled in me and
leaving a bright, empty garment which

only God can wear, and wear out.

How the Guru Eats My Karma

Lovers, there is a debt to the Guru
which money can't pay, it requires
a finer coin much dearer to come by;
one must suffer.
Only the Guru knows when one has
acquired such a coin in her purse.

One day I am meeting the Guru for lunch.
One of His disciples comes stumbling in with
a heavy box which contains a marble Buddha.
The Guru never wastes time; time is money.
Are you ready for another Sacred artifact? He
says, and right there I know I am cornered

like a rat caught in the bread closet. Food
at the Guru's table is never cheap. Yes, I say,
knowing full well what I am in for. The disciple
strains to lift out an antique white marble Buddha
that weighs about a thimbleful of my karma,
for that is the debt we are talking about here.

How much, I ask? He names a price which is
way more than I want to pay. It takes my breath
away and I sit there burning in it, dying. He is
offering me a chance to bear more of His burden
than I have been able to carry before; He knows
I have the coin in my purse.

(continues with stanza break)

Lovers, this is the debt from which money
cannot deliver us, this is the moment
we stop taking
and pick up our own Cross,
paying up,
working it off.

I Am the Guru's Boy

You can have your God and I am sure
He must be a fine fellow indeed
but I have used up all my means trying to cure
a broken heart and now I am in desperate need

of a Friend who can steer me right
and bring your God down to where my feet
are standing on the ground; I am in a fight
for my life here and the Guru alone will not retreat

from my madness so I am the Guru's boy and
I have all my eggs in His basket. If He goes down
then I go with Him. There's a certain joy and
gamble in that, refusing ego's burning crown

for the Guru's slavery. All I have now belongs
to the Guru. He gets my credits, I eat my wrongs.

Desire

Desire is a funny thing, Lovers.
Buddha said this about it:
Life is suffering;
all suffering is the result of desire.

How can this be, that the root
of all suffering is desire?
Consider the levee, that embodiment of desire,
an embankment of earth, stone, or concrete placed

to prevent the flooding of a body of water.
Naturally, it is placed only in a flood plain,
that natural overflow area of a river or stream
which allows for seasonal variations of water volume

and serves as a means for distribution of silt, which
prevents the riverbed from buildup of soil; thus
bottomlands are rich in alluvial soil, good farmland,
and so people farm there, settlements, then towns, finally

large cities develop, and they get wiped out by floods.
Men build levees, desiring to keep the river
at bay and protect their holdings.
Inevitably the levees give way, either undercut

by the action of moving water, or
overwhelmed by increased volume, or both.
They are rebuilt, higher, sturdier, always
in proportion to the desire of the settlers,

to avoid the flow of natural forces, always with one eye on the past, the other on the future, never here, never now. The result is inevitably more suffering. The solution is simple:

don't build on a flood plain, Lovers.

I Kiss My Master's Bare Feet

I had been around enough in the spiritual life
that when I first saw Your eyes Master
they drilled me;
they were bright blue
and utterly alive the way
2 young girls not yet broken with child
are alive as they dance down a crowded street
breasts unfettered, hips rolling in delight.

I was already broken with child
and wanted nothing more than to
kiss Your bare feet the way
I kiss my wife's, holding them to my face
and touching my lips to them with the
impossible tenderness of gratitude and remorse.
I will never do this for You because
You will not allow it and I lack the courage

but in this poem I fall down
beneath Your blue sky,
face in the dust and
I kiss Your bare feet.

Let Our Lives Be Dedicated To Your Feet
(Guru Gita)

Here I am writing a poem to the Guru's feet.
The audience for such a poem can be counted
on the fingers of one hand with enough left over
to give the finger to the rest of humanity.
I never dreamed it would come to this:
writing a poem adoring the Guru's feet.

Very well. I adore the Guru's feet.
I worship the Guru's feet.
I bow down and kiss the ground
the Guru's feet walk on.
I kiss the Guru's feet.

There. I've said it.
I love to kiss the Guru's feet.
I would rather kiss the Guru's feet
than kiss a woman's moist lips.

Alright then, maybe they are equal,
but you see how far I am gone
if those 2 are equal:

the Guru's feet and
a woman's moist lips,
the Sacred and the profane;

I'll let you guess which is which.

His Holy Feet

Consider the beauty of the feet and
the elegance of their surrender:
they have a sole
who bears all burdens without complaint,

goes wherever it is directed without question,
and labors unseen,
covered over with the body's concerns;
they are the root connection with the Earth,

the grounding force, the stability and
the balance point; when we
want to praise someone for her stability
we say, She has both feet on the ground.

My Master goes barefoot most everywhere,
a plain teaching demonstration about
simplicity, becoming as little children,
keeping in contact with one's roots;

His feet are Holy, we bow down to them,
kiss them, touch them with our foreheads.
When we love someone most profoundly,
as we love our Master, a great act of devotion

is to wash their feet, to rub their feet
when they are tired, and to kiss their feet;
intuitively we know the feet are Holy and
that we must be humble before them:

as the feet go, so is the Sole inclined.

The Beggar

Dearest, it's not my character to beg,
but there is nothing else that I can do
because I'm broken like a fragile egg
and so I come on bended knee to you

and plead with you dear Master do not make
a unified and stable man of me,
the kind who nothing in this world can break
because he has an inner unity

and has attained to oneness with you Lord.
Keep me ignorant, wretched, asinine;
surely one fool like me You can afford,
whose bad example makes the rest to shine

and if all others got to heaven before You
Beloved, who would be left to adore You?

Drinking From the Dharma Cup

Lovers, the Guru doesn't care whose cup
you drink the Dharma from, only that you
drink so much that you grow drunk

from its sweet wine and have to throw up
your precious beliefs all over the feet of the statue
of God in the park, the one the local monk

keeps cleaning the pigeons' Prasad from.
Once you have drunk from that sweet wine
you belong to the Guru, because He knows

that all of the varieties of good wine come
from the same vine; once drunk on the Divine,
it doesn't matter

in which vineyard the grape grows,
or which wine you drink of,
the Guru is all you can think of.

Drink From the Presence of Saints

Every drunk has his favorite wine.
The Saint Anjenaya is mine;
His grape is the sweetest on the vine.

In His Tavern we drunkards play
waiting for the Lord to take us away,
waiting for Anjenaya's Gaze to slay

our sobriety.
We drunks are the outcasts of society,
reviled by our Master's notoriety.

We are lost and beyond caring,
each night in His Tavern sharing
His overflowing cup and shamelessly staring

at His beautiful form.
In His Gaze we are reborn.
For one sip from His lips I risk the world's scorn.

Eaten Alive By Our Lord

I am being eaten alive by the Guru,
who is our Lord, Yogi Ramsuratkumar.
He is consuming the whole of me
the way a feral cat consumes a trapped bird,
slowly, delicately, feather
by talon by beak, leaving
nothing behind:
tailbone, cock & balls, teeth,
tongue, vertebrae, thoughts,
emotions, gestures and postures,
He is consuming the body
of habits and burning
in a smoking dung heap what
cannot be digested.

It is not what you think, it is
not as you imagine: it is
painful, it is ugly, it is
a horror;
every single stinking piece
of the madness
must be called forth and passed through,
seen and felt: there is
no other way.
When the Gospels say: This is my body,
eat of me; This is my blood, drink
in Remembrance of me, we
do not take this literally.
It is a fact. Beware,

all you who enter into the Tavern
of our Lord; the wine there
is purchased at a dear price:
all that we have for a single sip.
You can't get to heaven
with your clothes on.

The Dangerous Prayer
(for Regina)

58 years I have done it all my own way
and it has led me nowhere. So now I pray
for You to break me
Master, take me

and make me Your slave. Destroy
this self and turn me into Your serving boy,
one who is given small, menial tasks
and leaps to assist when his Master asks

for some trivial thing. I pray dear Master
that You make me Your footprint in the dust after
You have passed by; make me the sandals on Your feet
so that I might always kiss Your sweet

skin;
let shameless adoration be my only sin.

The Umbrella

Mister Lee is at the Ashram of His Master in India
with 16 of His disciples in hand. He is accompanied
by Purna, His old disciple who is a fine Teacher
Himself with students of His own. And it is Purna
I wish to speak of here, for His teaching demonstration
of a thing He learned from His Master, Mister Lee.

A group of male disciples is gathered around Mister Lee
at the gate of Yogi Ramsuratkumar's Ashram. It is
a dark day, pouring down rain and the photographer
is about to take a picture of the scene. The men
are in various poses of slouch; all eyes in the line of men,
including Mister Lee's, are on the photographer,

save one man:
Purna.
Purna's eyes are looking straight ahead and
it is obvious why. He stands next to Mister Lee and
without being obvious about it or looking right at Him,
all of His Attention is on His Master.

With his left hand in an awkward position,
He holds the umbrella over Mister Lee who is
smiling, peaceful and composed next to His
faithful disciple who is
soaking wet, in a painful position, and
utterly attentive, standing in an upright posture,

eyes alert and straight ahead.
It is clear that Mister Lee is pleased
and grateful.

Mister Lee's Jalali Lila

Jalali in Urdu means fierce and wrathful, usually
describing a mood or phase, a bhava,
which a Master will animate for a time,
months or even years, or momentarily.
Mister Lee's Jalali phase is a beautiful lila,
God using Its devotee Mister Lee to play
a melody upon the finely tuned strings of
Mister Lee's disciples: I play, you dance,

is the way this works with a Master
and His disciples. Those who are attuned,
love and delight in this fierce wrath and those
who are not are burned,
their egos ashen like their faces when
the Master's wrath is turned upon them.
Such a display is not always outward,
don't make that mistake Lovers. One time

I spoke up out of place in a Sacred space
which Mister Lee had created, smashing
this fragile chamber like a clumsy bum
dropping the wine on the pavement when
it is passed to him in a sack, so that
the other bums are horrified and
will not speak to him. That
is exactly what Mister Lee did,

He did not speak to me for the rest
of my visit; the suffering
of my shame was deep and burned away
lifetimes of arrogance and mindless babble:

this is what is meant by Jalali, Lovers; this
is tantric wrath, energy held in reserve,
out of sight, just below the boil while
the Lover burns.

The Path of Doubt

One disciple betrayed, another
denied, a third loved and then
there was Thomas, who doubted.
There is much misunderstanding
about the path of Doubt.

Doubt is the slow path to God, but
it is sure, not fooled by charlatans or
taken in by true-believers. It is scientific:
it takes the Dharma, tests it, observes
the results closely, then draws conclusions

based on the direct evidence of experience.
This is the awakening of real intelligence.
Thomas was surrounded by true-believers, but
he stayed with Jesus through the crucifixion
when many of the believers had fled.

When Jesus appeared in His Second Body
it was Thomas who refused to believe
until he stuck his fingers in the wounds.
Only then did he abandon all doubt and
surrender to the proof at hand, when

he had his Master's blood on his hands and
experienced his Master's suffering
in his own body.
He did not doubt his Master; he doubted
his own willingness to believe.

Make A Silk Purse Out of an Idiot's Heart

I have given my life without question
to every passing mood no matter
how vile and wretched, how full
of darkness and despair; I have

given my body to sorrows
of every dark and deepening shade and
to the thoughts which spawned them.
Lovers, you cannot imagine my delight

to at last lay down this life
for the Beloved whose kindness never fails,
whose Mercy is eternal and whose generosity
is so great He cannot give away His Father's

Blessings fast enough, heaping them upon us,
showering us, filling our hearts so they brim over
like a spring after heavy rain. I know
my heart is soiled, patched and worn Beloved,

still I beg You, take it and make of it a silk purse,
something to carry Your Father's coins in
so every time You spend His Blessings You reach
for my heart and hold it in Your hands and

the coins spill from it to feed the poor
and fill the Beggar's bowl to overflowing.

The Simple Path to Salvation

My Master says that He lacks devotion and,
although it appears to be otherwise
in the face of His selfless service to His Guru's
relentless worldwide Work,
I know He is telling the truth because

I too am devoid of such fine feeling
so I know that dog when I sniff under its tail.
In the place of devotion, He says,
I give obedience; it is
what I can do.

So there is an opening for a man like me, but
it is not so easy.
I am arrogant, willful, and lazy,
totally resistant to the guidance of others
and would rather go to hell my way

than enter heaven at someone else's instruction.
So it has to be really simple for an Idiot like me
to have a chance and this is what it looks like:
Stop doing what irritates the Guru.
This is known as the simple path to salvation

by those who have not tried to do it.
For the rest of us, the blind,
the stupid, the lazy, the pimps and whores
of sleep who think we are hot shit and know
something, anything, this is known as

nailing yourself to your own cross.

The Present Is the Source of All Creation

I am in love with all the simple things,
the hidden beauty that the moment brings,
the secrets that the present can reveal,
the joy that going slow can make me feel.

I have been bound by chains forged in the mind
which rules by fear and crushes all that's kind;
it thrives on making simple things complex
which drives the train of thoughts until it wrecks.

Now I put one slow foot before another
and treat each precious moment as my mother,
worshipping it and holding it so dear
because it brings my loving Master near.

The present is the source of all creation
and it is found through bodily sensation;
such a simple path to perfect ease,
to walk with mindful care among the trees

and find my patient Master waiting there
as if my sore Heart were His only care.
When I grow still He always comes to me;
He takes my hand and keeps me company.

You may curse such foolish poetry
which has no art or graceful symmetry.
I write for One whose Love has conquered death;
it is His Name I praise with every breath.

What A "Yes" To the Master Looks Like

At Darshan one night
Mister Lee described what a real "Yes"
looks like
when he makes a request of a student.

No facial change, He said.
No bodily shift,
no comment, question or hesitation,
no reaction.

The very next night after dinner,
He came and asked me if I would
take some books with me to Los Angeles
to be delivered to His students.

Yes…but, I said and
it doesn't matter what came next
after that instant of self-doubt because
it wasn't the books,

I never saw the books.
Such a simple request and
such a Holy burning shame
at not getting the job done.

I can talk all I want
about serving the Master but
if I'm not on full alert when He speaks,
it doesn't mean a damn thing.

The Power of Aim

Without an Aim, when my Master calls
I can miss my chance to serve.
It varies from moment to moment, the defense
of my inner position, but Aim falls
upon a higher center, one that does not swerve
from duty, a thing in me without pretense

which is capable of feeling when the Master speaks
and can respond to the urgency of my Aim.
When He speaks, if I am lost in inner consideration
then there is no Presence in me to feel Him, only leaks
and loss of force. But it is not the same
if my Aim's to serve, and I call on it without hesitation.

Then my Master's voice sounds within my Heart
and though He's worlds away, we never are apart.

Once the Horse Escapes

It is never wise to give your mouth to strangers
or your lips to those whose hearts you do not know;
a thoughtful reticence makes words grow stronger,
you govern mind and tongue and don't allow

a baseless rumor to pass through either door.
If one thing only governs thought and speech,
let it be kindness; the wise abhor and fear
a careless, cruel tongue for the harm it does, which

once spoken cannot easily be undone.
Once the horse escapes the confines of the barn,
it wastes the breath to wish he were not gone
and curse the day that he was ever born;

instead you walk the dirt path to the pond
and pray he is unharmed and will be found
before dark falls and wolves can take him down.
You swear from here on in to keep him penned.

Faith

In North Dakota in the winter time
blizzards can kill and
quickly, so

in order to save livestock, farmers
ventured into the blinding cruelty, the
ripping, tearing shark's teeth of the storm,

with a rope tied around their waist and
the wife holds one end of it inside
the house, the heart, the hand, the

faith
that when the rope goes slack
the man

still lives and will
come back
alive;

it is that way
exactly
with the Guru.

The Only Grace Is Bad Poetry

I used to think that Shakespeare was as good as it gets
in English poetry. Then I ran into Charles Bukowski,
a bum of no merit in the pecking order, a man
whose only claim to greatness was he told the truth
no matter how bad it made him look. All of a sudden
my ideas of what made for greatness in poetry
were in ruins.

But I did not count on meeting up with that bad poet
Mister Lee. He is as bad a poet as any who ever lived
and I stand in His lineage.
I stand upon His shoulders.
He is the foundation upon which we bad poets stand.
I once was a good poet, many said so but
it was no good for me.

Now, thanks to my dearest Master, I write this
dreadful drivel, because I cannot praise Him
enough or stop speaking of what He does for me
inside where no one can see. Dearest Master,
You have performed a miracle and the only way
I can let people see it is to allow You to make me
a bad poet just like You.

I adore this bad poetry which throws itself
on its face in the dust
at Your dear, Beloved feet and I can't stop
writing this drivel to save my Soul. Anyone
can be a good poet, they are burning
in all of the universities of hell, but
poetry this bad comes by Your Grace alone.

When I Sit Down To Write

Now when I sit down to write
no matter what subject arises before me,
You stand revealed Master and I can
barely think of anything else.
I was a man drowning in sorrows,
barely able to keep my head above water,
pulled down constantly into the dark current
and unable to rise.
You threw me the rope and You pulled me
onto dry land where I lay stunned and
barely alive while You tended to me
the way a mother caresses and sings to her
sick child until the fever goes from his eyes
and he can take crumbs from her fingers.
I once was lost the way the bums in the
Bowery chapels sing about, the way I have seen
wandering dogs search for the familiar scent.
I don't care anymore for the good poem
or the grand prize.
Now when I sit down to write I want only
to praise You in a humble voice the way
a sick child praises his Mother
for the cool rag she places
upon his fevered brow.

The Body of Silence

There is another body within this flesh
which can be sensed if one is
very delicate and full of Attention.
I call it the Body of Silence

into which the Being may move at any time
as a turtle with a single, simple move
goes from outside to within its shell.
This move is subtle, an inner sensation

and once there, the Being is a Silent Witness
to the simplest, smallest movement
of thought or emotion or tendency
from anywhere within the body.

The subtlest of thoughts
and the Being within the Body of Silence
sees it as a general upon a far hill
sees the movement of his troops;

there is noise, bloodshed, cries from below
and the general does not move or speak.
This is the Body of Silence:
clothed in understanding,

it knows Itself
and is not swayed by desire.
In the Silence the Being finds Itself;
in the Silence It is hidden out in the open

where Death cannot find it.

A Quiet Place
(L. Bernstein)

What we long for
awaits us within, but
something must loosen its hold
on our Attention; that ravenous scold
we call the mind covers over the quiet
with a riot of words, the thinking
never ceases.

But when the mind releases its grip
through careful and unceasing vigilance,
because it cannot stand to be seen
in the clear light of scrutiny,
something emerges from the cacophony
and stands revealed;
though long concealed by the noise,

the immeasurable Silence is poised
and elegant, voluptuous in its quiet praise
of emptiness, articulate and discreet
in the sweetness of its own
unutterable music, complete in itself
as if God created, and then paused,
lingered, exhaled, and only then was pleased.

The Silence of the Temple Bell

It is just after the ringing,
when a depth is touched within and
the inner note goes on, perhaps

for a very long time, one octave,
then another, a crossing over
into the exact, the real, the ever-close,

always present innermost Silence
from which all form and motion
arise, that vast ocean of repose

and solitude. The bell rings,
the monks on their cushions arise,
but something can go on, can remain

which comes from Stillness and brings
an inner calm; even when there is surprise
or alarm, a gentle hand upon the rein

holds the startled horse steady so it goes
surefooted on the path without a stumble.
There is the sounding of the bell and

there is the moment before, the moment
after, the long pause between
the first breath and the last.

For Whom the Temple Bells Chime

It is high plains desert, wind swept and
baked by Sun, very little rain though
on the day we placed Him on this spot,
double-rainbow all day long, ending
in the valley where He lay. So,
there is that to baffle reason, but
there is no excess here usually, everything
has its place and stays in it, nothing
is wasted, everything is precious.
Mister Lee was like that, precise and aware,
He knew His place and stayed in it,
serving to the end, nothing wasted,
only what was necessary.

In this desert now, His Ashram is in bloom,
wells find water, Temples rise, He prowls
with the lizards on the heated stone,
in the rocky valleys He is seen,
His footprints leave impressions in the sand,
He is risen like One who has mastered death.
No excess; He is in every breath,
He is the shadow where we stand,
He is the silence of the night, serene
but so we know we're not alone
He wakes us with Coyote howls.
He is not contained by a mere tomb;
for Him it is like a second womb

(continues with stanza break)

from which He emerges reborn in those who
serve Him, the anointed ones, the chosen few
who know their place and stay in it;
by Grace alone they live, minute-to-minute,
one breath at a time;
they know for Whom the Temple bells chime.

The Function of Conscience

I am sitting beneath a Japanese Red Maple
next to a pond, flicking bread crumbs to
the orange carp who swarm and tussle
for each crumb until suddenly,

floating into their midst in a
smooth elegant glide comes a white Carp and
the whole school shears off in 2 neat columns
as if on command, as if there were

a ghost in their midst, as if
the White Queen of the Carp had entered and
they made a path for her to my feet.
When I threw her a tasty morsel, all of them

held back like well trained dogs, their flanks
trembling with the discipline of waiting while
she cut cleanly for it, took her time consuming it,
then disappeared.

In a flash, they massed and swarmed the next crumbs.
All discipline vanished, like humans in a crowd when
someone yells, Lynch him! A rope appears and they
begin to look around for someone to sacrifice.

When the Queen retreats, hunger alone remains.

Who Are We And Why Are We Here?
(for Trungpa Rinpoche)

What do you imagine we are, if not Souls and
what do you imagine a Soul to be
if not an Angelic Being, come from a far-off place?

And if that much is so, then what on Earth
could our purpose be for coming here, if not
to learn what it means to love?

I don't mean sentimental love, not romance but
the hard labor kind of love that takes guts and gets its
hands dirty working the soil of forgiveness and

allows the heart to be broken over and over because
that's the only way to let love penetrate to where
the Soul bathes in the blood of its suffering.

What do you imagine is gained by such suffering
if not the Sacred Heart of Mercy, an Angelic Being
so tough, so seasoned by the agony of the flesh,

that it can forgive anything, can repay any offense,
no matter how great, with kindness? And
if kindness doesn't work,

the Soul whose broken heart has been
annihilated in the Sacred Heart of Mercy
tries more kindness.

One Day It Will Please Us To Remember This
(for Chandrika)

The years shatter and then they scatter
like rain drops on a hot stone.
This white hair suits you;
you wear it the way a young woman
wears her first prom dress, filling it out,
getting used to the newness of this beauty.

It rained all day today, cooling the night air.
This new ache in knee and wrist I am still
getting used to as I am to the presence of joy.
It left me when I lost my daughters' kisses
and now you bring it so I drink my daily fill;
it satisfies. I am getting used to deserving you.

We love to walk holding hands, pausing
to kiss and embrace. Aging makes it clear
how brief this sweetness, how precious the fleeting
joy which runs through us like sand through a glass
and leaves an ache in the heart because
we love in the shadow of our death;

such a slender sorrow is this tender dying,
that tomorrow will be time enough for crying.

The 3 Messengers of God

Buddha says God sends us
3 messengers to remind us
of who we are, and
where the Soul resides.

i. Old Age

She who clings to the body rages
against the thief who steals her beauty;
time scars her face as she ages;
she rouges her cheeks and cries out
as the bloom of youth flees and
her impending doom brings her to her knees.
Where once she was young and fair,
now she spends her days in prayer.

ii. Sickness

Sickness moves her into the Soul's domain;
freed from the body's greed by pain,
Mercy falls like gentle rain
upon the lined and upturned face;
the furrowed brow smoothes, leaves no trace
of sorrow in the dwindling space
which the vanishing life now occupies;
Grace descends, helps the broken Soul rise.

iii. Death

The Soul is a mystery from above, and
it blooms from the body's stillness
to fill the rooms with love
which once were rank with illness;
there is a kind of hush, as if something
was poised to make a great leap
into the present, that vast and starry deep.
Those not freed are left to weep.

For she who evolves, disappears somehow,
dissolves into the here and now,
these 3 are merely passers-by;
she is not moved by them, she does not die.

Mister Lee: the Good Mother

He is like our Earth, which is
the Feminine Principle in our system,
the Good Mother; He nurtures us all,
holding us close to His breast, feeding and
clothing us, providing salve and balm
for our wounds, unconditionally and
without regard for Himself Loving us;
He gives us birth and new life,
teaches us with the Patience of a Saint,
leaving none behind, holding out
His hand to us, gently and kindly
showing us the way; His reprimand
is gentle, His Rod unsparing but
skillfully and carefully and wisely
wielded so as to spoil no child;
His Staff, like a Good shepherd's,
comforts us, saves us from the rocky
and the thorny crevices, protects us
when hungry wolves circle and sniff;
even when we walk through that valley
whose shadow is Death, He does not betray
or abandon us; His Goodness and Mercy
sustain us all the days of our lives;
His inner countenance is as Still Waters
and He beckons us to lie down beside Him
and there to slake our Soul's thirst and
be restored; we dwell in His House, eat
His bread, drink from His bottomless cup
and nurse until we are grown and able
to stand alone without His gentle hand;
He is the Good Mother.

Mother Guru's Lullaby

Oh my Love, do not dare sleep
for in Awareness I will keep
you safe, protected from all harm;
in My Presence it is warm
and Death will never find you there.
I Am That which is Aware,
so my Love do not despair
if you cannot find Me anywhere;
your Longing is My answering prayer,
I Am the tears which you now weep
and the Force which lifts your arm
to dry them. I Am the tears upon your cheek,
they are the One for which you seek,
your broken Heart is my reply,
I Am your Breath and broken Sigh.
In you I Am both Still and Meek
but shelter you in raging storm
and comfort when you come to die;
your weeping is My lullaby.
Oh my Love, do not dare sleep,
the Wolf of Death forever creeps
always closer to my sheep,
but they are saved who Remember Me.
Lost and torn are they who slumber,
they will not find the Bridal Chamber,
the Wolf will count them in His number.
Keep my Name forever on your breath
and I will save you from the Wolf of Death.

Nocturne for Yogi Ramsuratkumar

Last night late You came to me
when there was no star I could see
and the Moon was hidden in the rain.
Down from the unforgiving sky
to soothe my broken-hearted pain
and ease my mournful begging cry
Your Grace and Mercy sweetly came,
and I remembered Your dear Name.
Oh Master how it soothed my Heart
and comforted my ancient hurt
that though You seemed a world apart,
You were nearer than the dirt
which hungered for the rain, the way
I'm praying for that Blessed day
when You so hunger from above
that You consume me in Your Love.

EPILOGUE:

The Way of Attention

The Way of Attention

Buddha says that 3 actions determine life.

i. breath
The wise woman observes her breath, conserves it,
follows it as the shadow follows the body,
is reserved, speaks only when necessary;
her speaking follows the 4 Imperatives:
kind, truthful, helpful, necessary, otherwise
she keeps her own counsel;
this is mastery of tongue.

ii. impressions
The wise woman observes impressions
without judgment or clinging,
impersonally the way the Sun
shines on all living things without favor;
she guards the impression she leaves with others,
showing only those feathers
suitable to the occasion;
she shows all her feathers only with good reason,
to birds of her own kind, everything in its season;
this is mastery of mood.

iii. sensations
The wise woman observes her body, studies its functions
and tames them the way the hunter
tames a good dog to follow her lead;
taming the senses, she is freed of excess,
practices moderation in all things, no need
to indulge in drifting thoughts, moods,
or the shifting desires of the body;
this is mastery of the form.   (continues with stanza break)

Buddha says that the total cessation of the 3 actions defines death. It is a wise woman who has mastered tongue, mood and form; she has mastered Attention, over which death has no dominion. She alone is free.

AFTERWORD:
Mother Guru

"Prayer is only praise, the selfless
    glorification, in words, mood or
gesture, of You, our King and Lord,
    our Guru and Mother…" (355. 14 March, 2010)

"And as for Adoration, well that
    is…pouring out of me like the ever-present
Praise of You, You, our Light,
    our God, our Mother…" (350. 7 March, 2010)

"I Your Minister of Praise, bow
    to Your Motherly Care and Concern…" (233. 16 Dec. 2009)

"You are like a mother,
    knowing when discipline is needed…" (200. Nov. 19, 09 v.)

"You, in Your great Mercy
    and infinite generosity, in
Your Radiant Grace and
    Motherly care for Your infants,
have given us Your Name…" (130. 19 November 2008 i.)

(from: Lee Lozowick, *Intimate Secrets of a True Heart Son*. Chino
Valley, AZ: Hohm Press, 2012.)

୬

"All under heaven have a common beginning.
This beginning is the Mother of the world.
    Having known the Mother…
we should go back and hold on to the Mother." (Lao Tsu. *Tao
    Te Ching*. Sutra 52.)

"There was something formless and perfect
    before the universe was born...
It is the Mother of the universe." (Lao Tsu. Sutra 25.)

"But wherein I am most different from others is
    in knowing to take sustenance from the great Mother!"
    (Lao Tsu. Sutra 20.)

"The spirit that never dies
    is called the mysterious feminine.
Although she becomes the whole universe,
    her immaculate purity is never lost.
Although she assumes countless forms,
    her true identity remains intact." (Lao Tsu. Sutra 6.)

(from: Wayne Dyer. *Living the Wisdom of the Tao.* Carlsbad, CA: Hay House, 2007)

INDEX OF FIRST LINES

Other HOHM PRESS Titles by Red Hawk

THE WAY OF POWER
by Red Hawk

"This is such a strong book. Red Hawk is like Whitman: he says what he sees..." – the late William Packard, editor, *New York Quarterly*.

"Red Hawk is a true poet whose work has strong, credible feelings and excellent timing." – Richard Wilbur, U.S. Poet Laureate and Pulitzer Prize winner.

"This collection continually surprises with insights that sometimes stop the breath." – Miller Williams, winner of 1995 Academy Award of the Academy of American Poets.

Paper, 96 pages, $10   ISBN: 978-0-934252-64-5

• • •

THE ART OF DYING
by Red Hawk

Red Hawk's poetry cuts close to the bone whether he is telling humorous tales or indicting the status-quo throughout the culture. Touching upon themes of life and death, power, devotion and adoration, these ninety new poems reveal the poet's deep concern for all of life, and particularly for the needs of women, children and the earth.

"An eye-opener; spiritual, native, populist. Red Hawk's is a powerful, wise, and down-home voice." – Gary Snyder

Paper, 132 pages, $12   ISBN: 978-0-934252-93-5

To Order: 800-381-2700
Or, visit our website at www.hohmpress.com

Other HOHM PRESS Titles by Red Hawk

WRECKAGE WITH A BEATING HEART
by Red Hawk

"Red Hawk's work puts us all in the line-up...We're all guilty, and Red Hawk himself is standing next to us." – Hayden Carruth, winner of the National Book Award, 1996.

This collection of over 250 new poems is Red Hawk's magnum opus, revealing the enormous range of his abilities in both free verse and sonnet forms. Red Hawk views the world with compassion tinged by outrage. He speaks with eloquence and raw power about all that he sees, including sex, death, hypocrisy and war as well as his own failures, and his life-altering remorse of conscience.

Paper, 300 pages, $16.95   ISBN: 978-1-890772-50-5

• • •

SELF OBSERVATION ~ THE AWAKENING OF CONSCIENCE
An Owner's Manual
by Red Hawk

This book is an in-depth examination of the much needed process of "self" study known as self observation. It offers the most direct, non-pharmaceutical means of healing the attention dysfunction which plagues contemporary culture. Self observation, the author asserts, is the most ancient, scientific, and proven means to develop conscience, this crucial inner guide to awakening and a moral life. This book is for the lay-reader, both the beginner and the advanced student of self observation. No other book on the market examines this practice in such detail. There are hundreds of books on self-help and meditation, but almost none on self-study via self observation, and none with the depth of analysis, wealth of explication, and richness of experience that this book offers.

Paper, 160 pages, $14.95   ISBN: 978-1-890772-92-5

To Order: 800-381-2700
Or, visit our website at www.hohmpress.com

Other Titles of Interest from HOHM PRESS

GRACE AND MERCY IN HER WILD HAIR
Selected Poems to the Mother Goddess
by Ramprasad Sen
Translated by Leonard Nathan and Clinton Seely

Ramprasad Sen, a great devotee of the Mother Goddess, composed these passionate poems in 18th-century Bengal, India. His lyrics are songs of praise or sorrowful laments addressed to the great goddesses Kali and Tara, guardians of the cycles of birth and death.

Paper, 120 pages, $12   ISBN: 978-0-934252-94-2

• • •

NOBODY SON OF NOBODY
Poems of Shaikh Abu-Saeed Abil-Kheir
Renditions by Vraje Abramian

Anyone who has found a resonance with the love-intoxicated poetry of Rumi, must read the poetry of Shaikh Abil-Kheir. This renowned, but little known Sufi mystic of the 10th century preceded Rumi by over two hundred years on the same path of annihilation into God. This book contains translations and poetic renderings of 195 short selections from the original Farsi, the language in which Abil-Kheir wrote.

These poems deal with the longing for union with God, the desire to know the Real from the false, the inexpressible beauty of creation when seen through the eyes of Love, and the many attitudes of heart, mind and feeling that are necessary to those who would find the Beloved, The Friend, in this life.

Paper, 104 pages, $12.95   ISBN: 978-1-890772-08-6

To Order: 800-381-2700
Or, visit our website at www.hohmpress.com

Other Titles of Interest from HOHM PRESS

THIS HEAVENLY WINE
Renditions from the Divan-E Jami
by Vraje Abramian

Following in the footsteps of the Persian mystical poets Rumi, Hafez and Nizami, the timeless works in this collection express the poet's overwhelming devotion to and longing for the Divine Beloved. The author, Nooreddin Abdurrahman Ibn-e Ahmad-e Jami, referred to colloquially as Jami (Jaami) was born in eastern Khorasan, Iran in 1414 and died in 1492. Jami's poetry seethes with spiritual ardor without being sentimental. His themes are varied, but ultimately lead back to a singular teaching that the Divine is not separate from the one who seeks and loves.

Paper, 112 pages, $12.95   ISBN: 978-1-890772-56-7

. . .

EYE TO FORM IS ONLY LOVE
A Journal of 100 Days
by Traktung Yeshe Dorje

For 100 days, the author, a Rinpoche in the tradition of Vajrayana Buddhism, kept a journal of short reflections. Some mornings, the heartbreaking poetry of devotion, or essays in celebration of dawn, light, trees; on others, razor-like distinctions about the nature of the mind, challenges to conventional views of seeing, or seething commentary on the shallowness of contemporary culture. Taken together, but in small considered bites, the entries provide a rare meal to any sincere practitioner who recognizes direct and authentic spiritual discourse.

Paper, 192 pages, $16.95   ISBN: 978-1-935387-29-9

To Order: 800-381-2700
Or, visit our website at www.hohmpress.com

Other Titles of Interest from HOHM PRESS

IN PRAISE OF RUMI
Lee Lozowick and others
Introduction by Regina Sara Ryan

Once a great Turkish scholar and theologian, Jelaluddin Rumi lost his heart to a wandering beggar, Shams E Tabriz, in whom he saw the face of God. His poetry extols his love and longing—for his beloved teacher, and for the Divine, alive in all things. *In Praise of Rumi* is a book of ecstatic poetry. It is an expression from the same chamber of the heart in which Rumi danced over 700 years ago. A book for those who know what it means to have a wounded heart, *In Praise of Rumi* celebrates the bittersweet pain and pleasure of tasting the raw Divine.

Paper, 80 pages, $9.95   ISBN: 978-0-934252-23-2

• • •

THE MIRROR OF THE SKY (BOOK AND CD)
Songs of the Bauls of Bengal
Translated by Deben Bhattacharya

Baul music today is prized by world musicologists, and Baul lyrics are treasured by readers of ecstatic and mystical poetry. Their music, lyrics and accompanying dance reflect the passion, the devotion and the iconoclastic freedom of this remarkable sect of musicians and lovers of the Divine, affectionately known as "God's troubadours."

The Mirror of the Sky is a translation of 204 songs, including an extensive introduction to the history and faith of the Bauls, and the composition of their music. It includes a CD of authentic Baul artists, recorded as much as forty years ago by Bhattacharya, a specialist in world music. The current CD is a rare presentation of this infrequently documented genre.

Paper, 288 pages, $24.95   ISBN: 978-0-934252-89-8
(includes CD)   CD sold separately, $16.95

To Order: 800-381-2700
Or, visit our website at www.hohmpress.com

HOHM PRESS Titles About Lee Lozowick

AS IT IS
A Year on the Road with a Tantric Teacher
by M. Young

A first-hand account of a one-year journey around the world in the company of Lee Lozowick (Mr. Lee Khepa Baul) a *tantric* teacher. This book catalogues the trials and wonders of day-to-day interactions between a teacher and his students, and presents a broad range of his teachings given in seminars from San Francisco, California to Rishikesh, India. *As It Is* considers the core principles of *tantra*, including non-duality, compassion (the Bodhisattva ideal), service to others, and transformation within daily life. Written as a narrative, this captivating book will appeal to practitioners of *any* spiritual path. Readers interested in a life of clarity, genuine creativity, wisdom and harmony will find this an invaluable resource.

Paper, 725 pages, 24 b&w photos, $29.95
ISBN: 978-0-934252-99-7

• • •

FACETS OF THE DIAMOND
The Wisdom of India
by James Capellini

Anyone who has ever felt the pull of India's spiritual heritage will find a treasure in this book. Contains rare photographs, brief biographic sketches and evocative quotes from contemporary spiritual teachers representing India's varied spiritual paths—from pure Advaita Vedanta (non-dualism) to the Hindu Vaisnava (Bhakti) devotional tradition. Highlights such well-known sages as Ramana Maharshi, Nityananda, and Shirdi Sai Baba as well as Yogi Ramsuratkumar, the Beggar-saint of Tiruvannamalai, South India, and his "true Heart Son," the American-born Lee Lozowick. Text in three languages—English, French, and German.

Cloth, 224 pages; 42 b&w photographs, $39.95
ISBN: 978-0-934252-53-9

To Order: 800-381-2700
Or, visit our website at www.hohmpress.com

HOHM PRESS Titles by Lee Lozowick

GETTING REAL
by Lee Lozowick

This book contains teachings from a seminar given in Mexico City in May 2006. Lee speaks about and actively demonstrates what it means to "get real," in contrast to the illusions of what it means to be "spiritual" in this day and age. His words are compassionate, but often brutally honest and humorous. He confronts the notions that keep his students and listeners stuck in their impractical visions of God or enlightened life. Instead, he encourages a relationship to reality that is characterized by integrity and discipline.

Paper, 160 pages, $16.95   ISBN: 978-1-890772-76-5

• • •

FEAST OR FAMINE
Teachings on Mind and Emotions
by Lee Lozowick

This book focuses on core issues related to human suffering: the mind that doesn't "Know Thyself," and the emotions that create terrifying imbalance and unhappiness. The author, a spiritual teacher for over 35 years, details the working of mind and emotions, offering practical interventions for when they are raging out of control. A practical handbook for meditators and anyone dedicated to "work on self." Lee Lozowick has written over twenty books, including: *Conscious Parenting; The Alchemy of Transformation;* and *The Alchemy of Love and Sex;* and has been translated and published in French, German, Spanish, Portuguese and other languages.

Paper, 256 pages, $19.95   ISBN: 978-1-890772-79-6

To Order: 800-381-2700
Or, visit our website at www.hohmpress.com

HOHM PRESS Titles by Lee Lozowick

DEATH OF A DISHONEST MAN
Poems and Prayers to Yogi Ramsuratkumar
by Lee Lozowick

This book is the living witness of a rare relationship between Master and disciple. It catalogs the devotional poetry—often written in the classic form of *ninda stuti*, "ironical praise"—of Lee Lozowick addressed to his Master, the Divine Beggar of Tiruvannamalai, Yogi Ramsuratkumar. Beginning with Lee's initial expressions of love and surrender in May 1979, hundreds more poems followed. This book contains those written through March 1998.

The essential poems and prayers are augmented with dharmic essays by other renowned individuals, including Arnaud Desjardins, Claudio Naranjo, Robert Svoboda and poet Andrew Schelling. Commentaries by some of Lee's students and dozens of Lee's song lyrics complete this bountiful offering.

Hardcover, 1276 pages, $108.00   ISBN: 978-0-934252-87-4

To Order: 800-381-2700
Or, visit our website at www.hohmpress.com

HOHM PRESS Titles by Lee Lozowick

GASPING FOR AIR IN A VACUUM
Poems and Prayers to Yogi Ramsuratkumar
by Lee Lozowick

Following in the format of *Death of a Dishonest Man* the poetry contained in this book spans the period from April 1998 through May 2004. Although Yogi Ramsuratkumar left his physical body in February 2001, Lee has continued to praise him day and night, and these poems reveal the union that flourishes and deepens between the Father and his "true heart son." To read these poems and prayers is to glimpse the reality of non-duality. Sometimes tender and intimate, at other times searing in their indictment of the fickleness of the Master's devotees, these poems promise an introduction to the house of prayer.

Essays included by Arnaud Desjardins, Llewellyn Vaughan-Lee, John Welwood, and others. Many more lyrics and two CDs of Lee's rock operas (*The Nine House of Mila* and *John T.*) included. A sumptuous feast.

Hardcover; 1099 pages; $145.00   ISBN: 978-1-890772-45-1

To Order: 800-381-2700
Or, visit our website at www.hohmpress.com

HOHM PRESS Titles About Yogi Ramsuratkumar

YOGI RAMSURATKUMAR
Under the Punnai Tree
by M. Young

Hohm Press's first full-length biography of the wondrous and blessed beggar of Tiruvannamalai. The firsthand accounts, anecdotes and teaching of this powerful biography transport the reader into the world of this contemporary saint. To be touched by the truth, beauty and love of this remarkable being will stir the heart's deepest longings. This book celebrates the inspiration of one rare individual who abandoned everything for the love of God.

Paper, 752 pages, 80+ photographs, $39.95
ISBN: 978-1-890772-34-5

• • •

ONLY GOD
A Biography of Yogi Ramsuratkumar
by Regina Sara Ryan

This powerful biography covers the life and teaching work of the contemporary beggar-saint Yogi Ramsuratkumar (1918-2001) who lived on the streets of Tiruvannamalai, India. "Only God" was his creed, and his approach to everyday life. It reflected his absolute faith in the one transcendent and all-pervasive unity which he affectionately called "My Father." The biography is an inspiring mix of storytelling, interviews and fact-finding.

Cloth, 832 pages, 30+ photos, $39.95   ISBN: 978-1-890772-35-2

To Order: 800-381-2700
Or, visit our website at www.hohmpress.com

ABOUT THE AUTHOR

RED HAWK was the Hodder Fellow at Princeton University and currently teaches at the University of Arkansas at Monticello. His other books are: *Self Observation: Awakening Conscience, An Owner's Man* (Hohm Press, 2009); *Raven's Paradise* (Bright Hill Press, 2010) winner 2008 Bright Hill Press poetry award; *Journey of the Medicine Man* (August House); *The Sioux Dog Dance* (Cleveland State University) nominated for the 1992 Pulitzer Prize in poetry; *The Way of Power* (1996); *The Art of Dying* (1999); and *Wreckage With a Beating Heart* (Hohm Press, 2005). He has published in such magazines as *The Atlantic, Poetry*, and *Kenyon Review*. He has given readings with Allen Ginsberg (1994), Rita Dove (1995), Miller Williams (1996), Tess Gallagher (1996), and Coleman Barks (2005), and more than seventy solo-readings in the United States.

Red Hawk is available for readings, lectures and workshops. He may be contacted at 824 N. Hyatt, Monticello, Arkansas, 71655; or via e-mail at: moorer@uamont.edu

ABOUT HOHM PRESS

HOHM PRESS is committed to publishing books that provide readers with alternatives to the materialistic values of the current culture, and promote self-awareness, the recognition of interdependence, and compassion. Our subject areas include parenting, transpersonal psychology, religious studies, women's studies, the arts and poetry.

Contact Information: Hohm Press, PO Box 4410, Chino Valley, Arizona, 86323; USA; 800-381-2700, or 928-636-3331; email: hppublisher@cableone.net

CPSIA information can be obtained at www.ICGtesting.com
Printed in the USA
BVOW07s0117100714

358316BV00001B/2/P